How to Profit from the Coming Boom in Gold

How to Profit from the Coming Boom in Gold

Jeffrey A. Nichols

McGraw-Hill, Inc.
New York   St. Louis   San Francisco   Auckland   Bogotá
Caracas   Lisbon   London   Madrid   Mexico   Milan
Montreal   New Delhi   Paris   San Juan   São Paulo
Singapore   Sydney   Tokyo   Toronto

Library of Congress Cataloging-in-Publication Data

Nichols, Jeffrey A.
    How to profit from the coming boom in gold / Jeffrey A. Nichols.
        p.   cm.
    ISBN 0-07-046488-X :
    1. Gold.   2. Investments.   3. Speculation.   I. Title.
HG293.N53   1992
332.63–dc20   92-4799
                                                           CIP

1 2 3 4 5 6 7 8 9 0   DOC/DOC   9 8 7 6 5 4 3 2

ISBN 0-07-046488-X

*The sponsoring editor for this book was Caroline Carney, the editing supervisor
was Fred Dahl, and the production supervisor was Donald F. Schmidt. It was
set in Baskerville by Inkwell Publishing Services.*

Printed and bound by R. R. Donnelley & Sons Company.

This publication is designed to provide accurate and authoritative information in regard to the subject matter covered. It is sold with the understanding that the publisher is not engaged in rendering legal, accounting, or
other professional service. If legal advice or other expert assistance is
required, the services of a competent professional person should be
sought.

> *—From a declaration of principles jointly adopted by a committee
> of the American Bar Association and a committee of publishers*

How to Profit from the Coming Boom in Gold
is dedicated to two very special people.

First to Suzan:
Without the love, encouragement, and
steadfast support of my wife,
I doubt very much that this book
would have been written.

And to Zachary:
The best little son in the world.

Contents

Part 2. The Investment Vehicles

Preface

I believe that gold will hit a new all-time high price sometime during the 1990s. This book explains how I reached this conclusion—and shows you how to profit through a wide variety of investment vehicles.

My bullish forecast does not rely on predictions of hyperinflation, financial crisis, collapsing currencies, stock market panic, or any of the other disasters that have been touted by gold bugs and other prophets of doom.

Instead, I build the bullish case for gold on a solid fundamental analysis, analysis which reveals diminishing supply and increasing demand for gold during the 1990s. These trends will result in gold price appreciation even without a resurgence of investor interest. However, once investors are convinced that a new bull market is underway, they will jump on the bandwagon and push gold to record heights.

In this book, I don't just talk about the gold boom. I also show you how to profit from this knowledge. You'll learn how to design your own personal gold investment program, one that suits your financial goals, your willingness to accept risk, and your overall investment portfolio. In addition, I'll tell you everything you need to know to invest and trade successfully in the whole range of gold-related vehicles—coins, bars, mining stocks, mutual funds, futures markets, and options. And we'll carefully examine the advantages, disadvantages, relative risks, and rewards for each investment category.

The proposition of this book is that the average investor has the opportunity to score big profits during the 1990s—and perhaps realize his or her dreams by making the right gold investment decisions.

Although I have written *How to Profit from the Coming Boom in Gold* for the average investor, I am sure it will prove equally, if not more valuable, to even the sophisticated investor, as well as the professional money manager and institutional investor.

Jeffrey A. Nichols

How to Profit from the Coming Boom in Gold

1
Introduction

I've been a gold analyst for nearly two decades, but I'm no gold bug. I witnessed the bull market of the 1970s and the bear market of the 1980s. I've made a living out of seeking the truth of the market—and sharing my views with clients: bullion dealers, gold mining companies, mints, institutional investors, and other major participants in this market around the world.

Now, I want to share with you some of the things I've learned along the way:

- Why I strongly believe that the gold price is heading significantly higher during the years ahead.
- What vehicles are available to you as an investor and speculator.
- How to use gold as a portfolio hedge.
- How to profit from the coming bull market.

To achieve my objectives, I'll carefully review gold's supply and demand fundamentals, which will provide the foundation for higher gold prices in the years ahead. Next, I'll introduce you to the various ways to invest in gold from coins and bullion to mining shares and mutual funds to options and futures. Finally, I'll give you some guidelines for investing and speculating. Throughout this book, my belief is that an educated investor can enjoy success in the world of gold.

A Sane and Sensible Investment

Gold bugs believe in gold, almost religiously. For the gold bug, bullion is the one secure asset in what they believe to be an insecure world. To be sure, over the decades and centuries, gold has proven itself to be the best store of wealth and insurance policy against political or economic upheaval. For people living in politically or economically unstable countries around the world, the metal continues to provide a financial safe haven that may not be available in other assets.

But for Americans, Western Europeans, Japanese, and others around the world, gold is merely one financial asset among many—stocks, bonds, money market instruments, and a wide range of sophisticated vehicles that provide individuals and institutions with the opportunity to hedge risks and take positions on everything from foreign currencies to crude oil to inflation itself.

Nevertheless, I believe that gold does have some special characteristics that warrant its inclusion in a well diversified and risk-averse portfolio. Completely apart from one's forecast for gold prices, there are solid arguments in favor of including some gold in any prudent investment program. One important premise of this book is that there is a place for gold and gold-related assets in virtually every American's savings and investment program. You don't have to be a wealthy or sophisticated individual investor or a large institutional investor to benefit from gold. Chapter 13—"The Gold-Plated Portfolio"—will explain how and why gold reduces risk in a portfolio and serves as an insurance policy against unexpected risks.

Gold—the Commodity

However, this book makes the case for gold during the 1990s, not so much as a financial asset, but as a commodity. Gold bugs have long built their bullish case for gold on a foundation of disaster—stock market disaster, bankrupt banks, accelerating inflation, collapsing currencies, wars, and so on. The last few years, if they have proven anything about gold, have shown that the market can no longer rely upon these sorts of events to significantly or sustainably boost gold into a higher trading range.

In early 1991, all at once, many of the gold bugs' dreams came true: war in the Persian Gulf, currency market turbulence, global bear markets in stocks and bonds, a doubling of oil prices, an epidemic of bank insolvencies in the United States. Yet the ultimate gold bug dream—higher gold prices—did not come true. Investors in North America and Western

Figure 1.1.

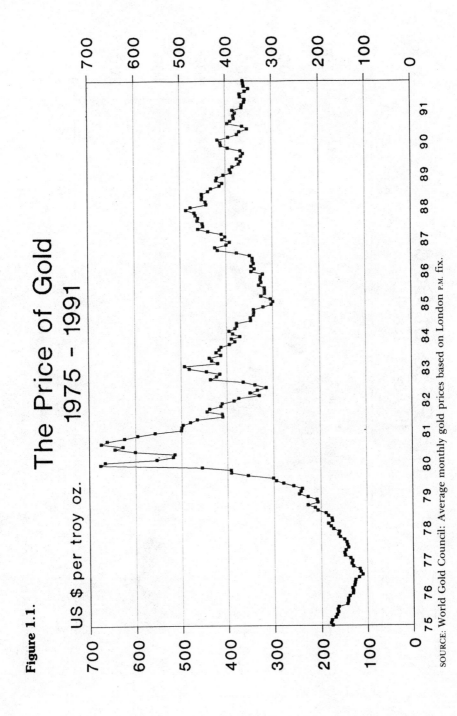

The Price of Gold
1975 – 1991

US $ per troy oz.

SOURCE: World Gold Council: Average monthly gold prices based on London P.M. fix.

Figure 1.2a.

The Price of Gold
1975 – 1991

US $ per troy oz.

DM per troy oz.

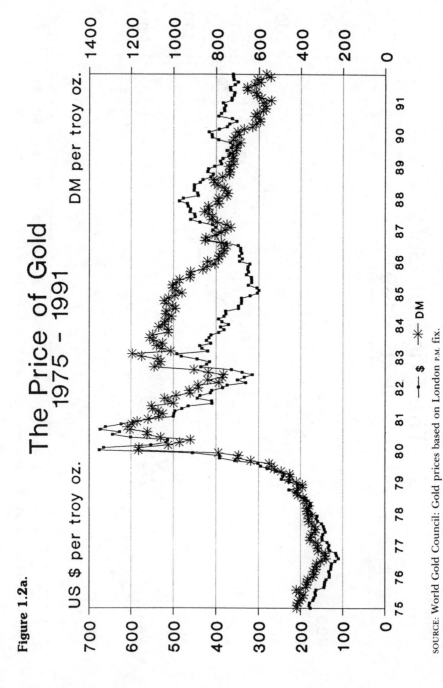

SOURCE: World Gold Council: Gold prices based on London P.M. fix.

6

Figure 1.2b.

The Price of Gold
1975 – 1991

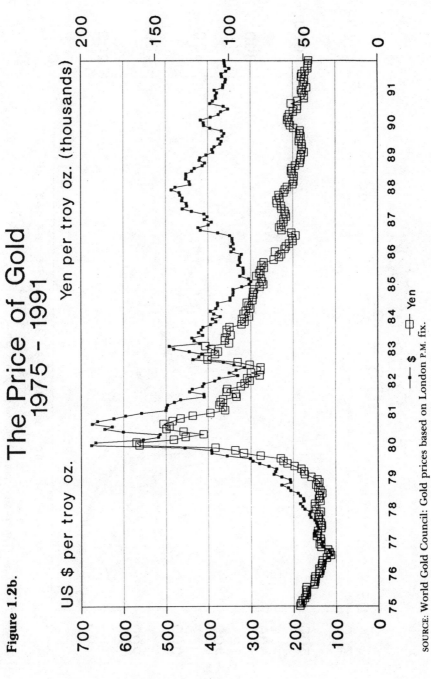

US $ per troy oz.

Yen per troy oz. (thousands)

— • — $ —□— Yen

SOURCE: World Gold Council: Gold prices based on London P.M. fix.

7

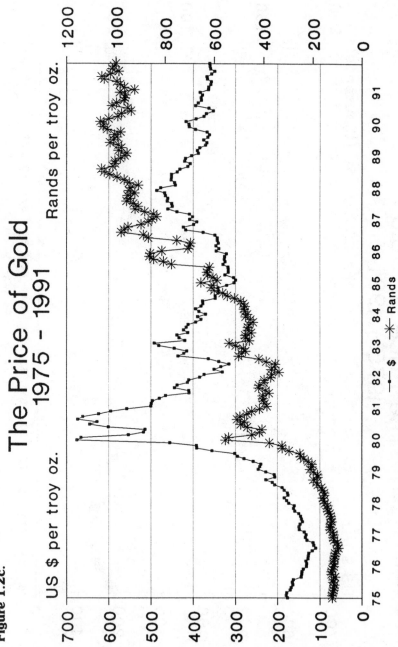

Figure 1.2c.

The Price of Gold
1975 – 1991

US $ per troy oz.

Rands per troy oz.

SOURCE: World Gold Council: Gold prices based on London P.M. fix.

$ — Rands ⁂

Europe continued to shun gold. Events, which years ago might have prompted a stampede of investor demand for the metal, now barely cause a yawn. Investors have found other ways to hedge the risks associated with these problems. Gold is no longer the only game in town, as it may have been a decade or two ago.

All this does not discredit the case for gold during the coming years. I believe that the price will move substantially higher, before the end of the decade surpassing the previous historical peak price of near $875 an ounce.* My bullish forecast is based on a solid foundation. Supplies of gold entering the market are already diminishing—and will continue to trend lower during the next few years. Meanwhile, demand for gold as a commodity for jewelry fabrication and other industrial uses has grown rapidly during the past few years—and this expansion will continue during the years ahead. Already, in the early to middle 1990s, jewelry and industrial demand will bump up against available supplies—and, inevitably, the metal's price must rise to maintain market equilibrium.

What's Ahead

The plan for the book is simple. Chapter 2 presents the bullish case for gold. In Chaps. 3 and 4, I'll review the historical and prospective trends in the key sectors of supply and demand which are the solid foundation upon which higher gold prices will be built. Chapters 5 and 6 review investment demand for gold from central banks and private investors, respectively. And, I will explain why investors will eventually return to the market, contributing significantly to a new and powerful bull market.

If you are already convinced or in a hurry to get started, you can skip to Part 2 where individual chapters review the basics of various gold investment vehicles. Use this section as a handbook or reference to buying bullion coins or physical gold, investing in gold mining equities and mutual funds, speculating in futures, and utilizing options.

Part 3 will help you design the best gold investment program to suit your own needs and temperament. Building a golden nest egg, dollar cost averaging, who should own mining equities and mutual funds, when to speculate and how to pyramid your profits are some of the topics covered. Specific advice for different types of investors is provided to help you decide how much to invest and which vehicles make the most sense.

---

*Throughout this book, unless otherwise noted, prices refer to the current month or "spot" price on New York's Commodity Exchange. On January 21, 1980 the spot price on COMEX touched an intraday high of $875 an ounce.

Whether you're a conservative investor seeking to minimize risk or an aggressive investor willing to take some risks in order to profit handsomely from the coming bull market, whether you are of modest means or wealthy, and whether you're a young adult or retiree, I'll give you some guidelines that will help you achieve your goals.

Gold investing can be a risky business when not done right. The best investor is an educated investor. Throughout this book, my aim is to help you preserve and create wealth for yourself without taking risks which are beyond your own means. Too many investors make mistakes and take risks that are not only beyond their means but that are avoidable by adhering to some sensible guidelines. Chapter 14 highlights the mistakes most frequently made by gold investors so that you can avoid them.

You will need to develop a sense of timing, particularly if you plan to take an aggressive approach to maximizing your profits during the coming bull market. Chapter 15 presents an introduction to technical analysis so that you can use charts and the other tools of the technician as guides to timing and market direction.

The gold market has a vocabulary all its own. The jargon of traders, miners, refiners, and investors need not be an impediment. Chapter 16 is a glossary of gold investment terms to help guide you from the A's to the Z's of the world of gold. Although at the end, this may be one of the most important chapters of the book and should serve as a lasting desk reference for the gold investor.

PART 1
The Fundamentals

2
The Bullish Case for Gold

Although gold is unlike any other commodity, serving equally as a monetary asset and store of value, it is the yellow metal's commodity-like characteristics—its fundamentals of supply and fabrication (noninvestment) demand—that promise to propel the price of gold to much higher levels during the mid-1990s.

Looking Back at the Bear Market

The 1980s were years of rising gold supply and, until late in the decade, stagnant or sluggish growth in jewelry and industrial demand for gold. These trends in supply and demand, in part a reaction to the superhigh prices early in the decade, were important factors contributing to the bear market that began in 1980 and continued into the early 1990s.

Three separate developments led to the rapid growth in supply during this period:

1. Mine production in North America and Australia grew extremely rapidly.

2. As I'll detail later, gold loans to finance project development and forward sales by mining companies* also added to available supplies.

3. Gold sales by the former Soviet Union accelerated in the late 1980s and reached a peak in 1991.

At the same time, tight monetary policies in the major industrial nations, high real interest rates and strong stock markets around the world, declining inflation, and rising confidence in the U.S. dollar as an international store of value and safe haven asset resulted in an investment climate that was hostile to gold. In this environment, investors—at least American and Western European investors—were content to hold competing financial assets such as stocks, bonds, and money market instruments where the returns seemed more assured.

Moreover, the declining trend in the gold price itself spawned further investor disinterest and ultimately led to the dishoarding of gold by many investors in the United States and Europe. And, as investor demand waned, the downtrend in the metal's price was reinforced and ultimately exaggerated.

Asian investors—who have a penchant for buying cheap—were, nevertheless, aggressive buyers during the past dozen years. While this may have provided temporary support at times to the gold price as it moved lower, the bargain basement nature of Far Eastern buying was not sufficient to reverse the downtrend.

A Period of Transition

The closing years of the 1980s and the early 1990s have been important transitional years in terms of gold supply and demand. Following years of rapid growth, the total annual supply of gold entering the market from mine production, East bloc sales, scrap recover (also known as secondary supply), and the hedging activities of mining companies actually peaked in 1991 at roughly 91 million ounces (about 2824 metric tons). During 1992 or 1993, total annual supplies entering the market will fall rapidly—reflecting, among other factors, the end of aggressive gold sales by the former Soviet Unioin and a leveling off in worldwide mine production. Importantly, the annual supply of gold during the decade of the nineties will continue to trend lower.

*These activities—the borrowing of gold by mining companies to finance project development and the trend toward increased forward sales—and their impact on the market are explained in Chapter 3.

A Note About the Statistics

Throughout this book, supply and demand statistics will be presented in troy ounces. Often, I will also report the data in equivalent metric tons.

Americans tend to think in ounces while the rest of the world works on the metric system where tons are the standard unit of account for gold supply and demand. For those with a calculator, 1 metric ton equals 32,151 troy ounces. More on units of measure can be found in the glossary.

Meanwhile, fabrication demand—that is demand by jewelry manufacturers and other industrial users—surged in the late 1980s. Jewelry demand alone has risen from about 44 million ounces (1369 tons) per year in 1986 and 1987 to well over 60 million ounces (1866 tons) a year in 1990 and 1991. In recent years, jewelry alone has consumed every ounce of gold produced by the world gold mining industry (excluding the East bloc). Other industrial users of gold—in electronics and dentistry, for example—consume another 8 million ounces (249 tons) or so a year.

Taken together, jewelry and other industrial demand amounted to roughly 74 million ounces (about 2302 tons) in 1991. At the same time, the annual supply from mine production, forward sales and gold loan transactions by mining companies, old scrap, and East bloc sales totaled roughly 91 million ounces (2830 tons). The difference—in the jargon of economists, the annual market surplus—is what is left over to satisfy net investment demand from the private sector and from central banks. This surplus can be seen on the bottom of Table 2.1 under the designation "Total Stock Changes."

The Shrinking Surplus   [Supply + Demand]

The main point you need to grasp here is that the surplus—total stock changes—peaked in 1988 near 29 million ounces (over 892 tons). By the beginning of the 1990s, the annual surplus had fallen sharply—to about 17 million ounces (486 tons) in 1990 and 1991.

When analysts talk about "tightening supply and demand fundamentals," what we really mean is that the surplus of gold available to satisfy net investment demand—from both the private sector as well as the official central bank sector—is shrinking. In commodity markets, shrinking surpluses or growing deficits are the catalysts to rising prices.

Table 2.1. The Supply and Demand for Gold
(million troy ounces)

	1986	1987	1988	1989	1990	1991*	1992*
Mine production							
South Africa	20.6	19.5	20.0	19.6	19.5	19.3	19.0
United States	3.8	5.0	6.5	8.3	9.3	9.6	10.1
Canada	3.4	3.7	4.3	5.1	5.3	5.5	5.3
Australia	2.4	3.6	5.0	6.2	7.8	7.2	6.0
Brazil	2.2	2.7	3.2	3.1	2.7	2.1	1.9
Other market economies	9.3	10.0	10.8	10.9	12.0	12.9	13.8
Total	**41.7**	**44.5**	**49.8**	**53.2**	**56.6**	**56.6**	**56.1**
Forward sales/gold loans	**2.7**	**3.5**	**15.0**	**10.0**	**5.5**	**6.0**	**4.0**
Old scrap	**12.5**	**11.0**	**10.0**	**9.0**	**10.5**	**8.5**	**8.0**
East bloc sales							
Soviet Union/CIS	9.6	4.6	7.4	10.3	12.9	16.1	3.2
China	2.7	2.8	2.9	2.9	3.0	3.0	3.0
North Korea	0.5	0.5	0.6	0.6	0.6	0.6	0.6
Total	**12.8**	**7.9**	**10.9**	**13.8**	**16.5**	**19.7**	**6.8**
Total supply	**69.7**	**66.9**	**85.7**	**86.0**	**89.1**	**90.8**	**74.9**
Industrial Use	**7.4**	**7.4**	**7.8**	**8.0**	**8.0**	**7.9**	**8.0**
Jewelry	**37.1**	**38.5**	**48.6**	**60.2**	**63.8**	**66.0**	**68.0**
Total Fabrication	**44.5**	**45.9**	**56.4**	**68.2**	**71.8**	**73.9**	**76.0**
Official purchases							
or sales (−)	**7.2**	**2.5**	**7.0**	**−5.0**	**0.0**	**−5.0**	**0.0**
Net private investment							
Coinage†	10.9	7.0	4.7	4.7	4.9	6.0	4.5
Bullion Surplus	7.1	11.5	17.6	18.1	12.4	15.9	−5.6
Total	**18.0**	**18.5**	**22.3**	**22.8**	**17.3**	**21.9**	**−1.1**
Total Stock Changes	**25.2**	**21.0**	**29.3**	**17.8**	**17.3**	**16.9**	**−1.1**

*APMA estimates for 1991 and projections for 1992. Copyright 1991—American Precious Metals Advisors, Inc. This table may not be reproduced in whole or in part without express permission of APMA.

†Includes bullion, commemorative, and imitation coins, medals, and medallions.

While the fundamentals were tightening from 1988 through the early 1990s, gold prices continued to slump. A paradox? Not at all. As long as investors as a group were willing to accept smaller additions each year to their accumulated gold holdings, gold prices may decline even though the surplus is diminishing.

Bullish Fundamentals

My forecast of higher gold prices during the mid-1990s is based on the absolute certainty that the annual supply of gold entering the market will continue to diminish over the years ahead, while jewelry and industrial

Figure 2.1. Gold's Tightening Fundamentals

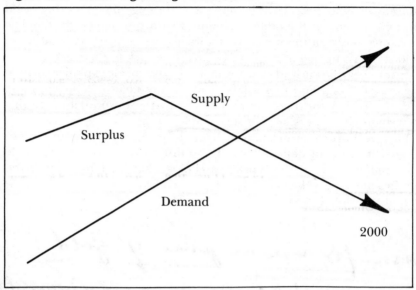

Supply

Surplus

Demand

2000

demand will continue to expand as long as the world economy is growing. As a result, the surplus will disappear altogether and will be replaced by a deficit—that is, unless the price moves significantly higher. Indeed, a higher price is the mechanism through which the market adjusts to maintain a balance between overall supply on the one hand and demand from both fabricators and investors on the other hand.

The following two chapters review the historical and prospective trends in each component of supply and fabrication demand so that you can see for yourself how the fundamentals of gold are changing.

Without any rise in the price of gold to balance the market, it is likely that the surplus will disappear sometime in the early to middle 1990s to be replaced with a deficit. In other words, fabrication demand will exceed supply—and dishoarding by investors and central banks would be necessary to satisfy the needs of jewelry manufacturers and other industrial users.

Indeed, this would be an unprecedented situation in the world of gold. Never—not even in ancient and biblical times—has the gold market been in deficit. From year to year over the millennia, there has always been a surplus of gold available to meet the world's investment and monetary demand for the metal. But this will change—unless prices rise sufficiently to alter these prospective fundamentals.

It is inconceivable that investors and central banks would—as a group—dishoard gold in sufficient quantities year after year to satisfy the needs of

Before the end of 1990's - unsustainable rise
(explosion) in price of gold.

20   The Fundamentals

the market. In fact, investment demand for gold will probably begin rising again—not necessarily because of worsening inflation, rising world tensions, or any of the other calamities that are supposed to stimulate investor interest in the metal. Investors like rising markets—and when gold starts rising again, it will draw investors back to the market.

In my view this will lead to an unstable, unsustainable explosive surge in the price of gold. Fortunes will be made by the smart gold investor and speculator—but fortunes will also be lost by those who fail to see that superhigh gold prices are not sustainable.

I'll have more to say in Chap. 6 about historical and prospective trends in gold investment demand. I will also discuss the psychology of gold investment. The mania and crowd psychology that develops among investors in a bull market is what will push gold to historic new highs before the end of this decade.

Reason for rise in price of gold:

Investors like rising prices (markets)
—and when gold starts rising again, it
will draw investors back to the
market.

a "unstable, [unsustainable] explosive
surge in the price of gold."

"... super high gold prices are
not sustainable."

3
Supply Trends

Introduction

The great bear market in gold began in January 1980, the moment after the metal touched its all-time high price near $875 an ounce. Contributing to the long-term downtrend in the metal's price was the rapid growth in supply throughout most of the decade. In fact, the quantity of gold entering the market each year rose from about 48 million ounces (1493 tons) in 1979 to roughly 90 million ounces (nearly 2800 tons) in 1991, the year of peak supplies. Over those 12 years, total supply grew at a compound annual rate of 5.4 percent.

But beginning in 1992, the aggregate amount of gold entering the market each year will begin to decline—and this downtrend will persist for years to come. The shrinkage of supply during the 1990s—in contrast to the rapid expansion which characterized much of the prior decade—is one reason why I'm bullish about gold's long-term prospects. Yet, most people don't understand that the trend in supply has already reversed.

In measuring annual supply, we are interested in the total amount of gold entering the market each year from all sources: mine production in the free market nations, secondary supply or scrap recovery, sales into the world market by Russia and other East bloc countries, and gold flows arising from the forward sales and bullion financing activities of mining companies.

For many, this may already be confusing. Bear with me, and by the end of this chapter you'll be an expert on the sources of gold supply. Let's look at each component of supply in turn—and I'll explain why the trend is down for the years ahead.

Mine Production

By far, mine production is the biggest source of gold entering the market. Excluding the former Soviet Union and other East bloc countries, which are accounted for separately, total mine production has risen from about 31 million ounces (964 tons) per year in the late 1970s to about 57 million ounces (1773 tons) in 1990. That's a growth rate of 5.7 percent a year.

The high price of gold prevailing in the late 1970s and early 1980s provided the impetus for increased gold mining exploration, development, and ultimately production. At the same time, advancements in the technology of exploration, mining, and metallurgical extraction techniques—particularly heap leaching—contributed to the gold rush of the 1980s. In contrast, the depressed price of the past few years has discouraged exploration and development activity—and the result will be lower mine output in future years.

The major national producers are South Africa, the United States, Canada, Australia, and Brazil. Table 3.1 presents annual production statistics for the top ten gold mining countries along with my projections

Table 3.1. Western World Gold Mine Production (million troy ounces)

	1980	1985	1990	1995*
South Africa	21.7	21.6	19.5	17.5
United States	1.0	2.6	9.3	10.0
Australia	0.5	1.9	7.8	4.5
Canada	1.7	2.9	5.3	4.5
Brazil	1.1	2.3	2.7	1.6
Philippines	0.7	1.2	1.2	1.4
Papua New Guinea	0.5	1.0	1.1	2.3
Columbia	0.5	0.8	1.0	1.2
Chile	0.3	0.7	0.9	1.5
Zimbabwe	0.4	0.5	0.6	0.9
Others	1.7	4.2	7.2	7.6
Total	30.1	39.7	56.6	53.0

SOURCES: Gold Fields Mineral Services Ltd, American Precious Metals Advisors, Inc.
*Forecast—American Precious Metals Advisors.

for each country's gold output in 1995. Two trends are apparent from this table: First, South African output has edged lower over the years—and will continue to ebb over the current decade. Second, gold production in a number of other countries exploded during the 1980s—but this growth is now reaching a plateau and will be trending lower during the middle 1990s. By 1995, world gold mine production is expected to decline to about 53.5 million ounces (1664 tons). This represents an average annual decline of about 1.3 percent per year during the first half of the decade, in stark contrast to the rapid growth experienced during the prior five-year period. If anything, these estimates for 1995 are generous—and actual output could turn out to be even lower.

South Africa

South Africa has long been the world's leading producer of gold. Despite the long-term downtrend in the country's gold output—which began in the early 1970s and is likely to persist for decades to come—South Africa will almost certainly retain the number one position among national gold producers for many, many years. Gold is crucial to South Africa, for over a century being the most important sector of the economy and the country's chief source of national wealth and foreign exchange.

The country's mines are unique in a number of features. The South African gold mines are generally much larger and much deeper than gold mines elsewhere around the world. Today much of the mining is at great depth, as much as 13,000 feet or more than 2 miles underground. At these extreme depths, the earth's temperature is unbearable, requiring major cooling systems to make work conditions barely tolerable. The gold is concentrated in narrow reefs or veins usually of 8 to 12 inches in width and the areas being mined are often little more than 3 feet high in order to minimize the removal of waste rock while leaving just enough room for a crew of miners to work.

Having visited a number of South African gold mines over the years, I can only marvel at the organizational and engineering accomplishments of the industry. Each mine is a major industrial complex. Many have underground work forces numbering in the tens of thousands to produce hundreds of thousands of ounces of gold a year. A handful actually produce more than a million ounces a year. Moving this quantity of men and their required supplies underground in two work shifts per day and raising the ton after ton of blasted rock to the surface for milling and processing is an enormous feat. On average, about 6 tons of rock must be moved to the surface to recover 1 ounce of gold.

6 T. of Rock = 1 oz gold.

This is hard work. One work shift general prepares an area of gold-containing rock for blasting, drilling, hour after hour, a series of holes that will later be filled with blasting explosives. These will be plugged with dynamite and detonated to break the rock into managable pieces which can be removed by another work crew and eventually moved to the surface. Meanwhile, other miners are busy maintaining the work areas, extending shafts and stopes, maintaining and repairing equipment, and providing a variety of other essential services.

Although there are some exceptions, many of the South African gold mines have moved from being the world's lowest cost producers in the 1970s and early 1980s to being among the highest cost producers today. This reversal of fortune reflects the depletion of higher grade ore reserves, the increasing underground depth of operations, and the continuing rapid rise in labor costs.

About one-third of the gold mines in South Africa have operating costs in the $350 to $370 an ounce range (see Table 10.6). Moreover, 11 mines with annual output of about 3.5 million ounces (109 tons) were operating at a loss—with working costs exceeding revenues—in 1990 and 1991. If we account for depreciation and other indirect costs, the industry's profit picture would look still more depressing.

As can be seen from Fig. 3.1, the South African gold mines have seen their cost structure rise and their profitability decline from one year to the next. The average gold recovery grade has fallen from over 0.4 ounces/ton in the early 1970s to just over 0.15 ounces/ton in the past few years. Meanwhile, the real operating cost—denominated in constant 1990 rands per ounce—has quadrupled over the same time period. As a result, the profit margin (the difference between the gold price and the operating cost)—also in real inflation-adjusted terms—has narrowed dramatically.

Two key trends are certain to continue influencing the direction of South African gold output: Ore grades will continue to fall and labor costs will continue to rise as the black mine workers seek economic equality within South Africa. As a result, South African production will continue to ebb over the years ahead—unless there is a substantial and lasting increase in the price of gold, an increase which would warrant the investment of billions of dollars to maintain or expand mine capacity and prove up new reserves.

North America and Australia

In contrast to the downtrend in South African output, gold production through 1990 continued to expand in most other countries around the world. But the rate of growth has been slowing and will soon reverse. In

Figure 3.1a. Factors affecting South African gold production: average gold recovery grade.

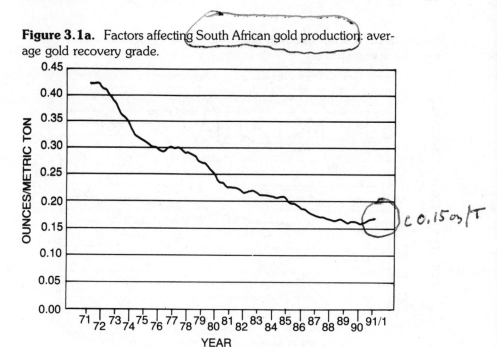

Figure 3.1b. Factors affecting South African gold production: real operating costs of gold (per ounce produced).

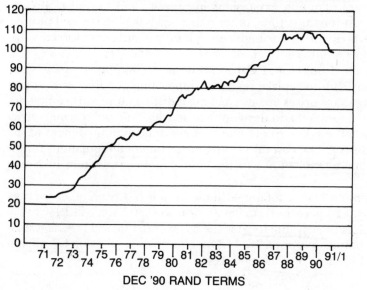

Figure 3.1c. Factors affecting South African gold production: gold price vs. operating costs.

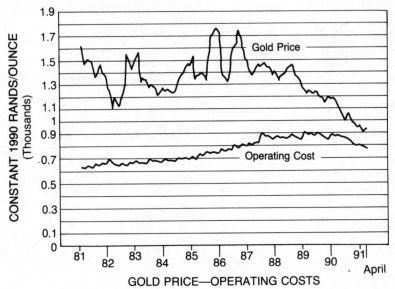

GOLD PRICE—OPERATING COSTS

fact, the number of new mines coming into production and the number of existing mines planning expansions in capacity and output is already decreasing. At the same time, other mines are reaching the end of their productive lives and some high-cost mines are suffering forced shut-downs thanks to low gold prices.

In the United States and Canada, the major mining companies are finding it difficult to replace reserves. Importantly, depressed gold and gold mining share prices are also making it difficult for many companies to finance exploration and development activity. And, increasingly strict environmental regulations are also proving to be an impediment to the mining industry. The cost of meeting environmental regulations is now adding about $20 an ounce to the cost of gold production in North America.

In the United States, total gold mine output has risen at an average annual rate of 23 percent from 980,000 ounces (30.5 tons) in 1980 to 9.6 million ounces (nearly 300 tons) in 1991. Over the same 11 years, Canadian gold output has risen by 11.5 percent per year from 1.7 million ounces in 1980 to 5.5 million ounces in 1991.

Heap Leaching

Total annual gold production in the United States and Canada will probably register little change over the next few years, falling from 15.4 million ounces (479 tons) in 1992 to about 14.5 million ounces (451 tons) in 1995. Although this is not a large decline, it represents a major turnabout from the rapid growth of the past several years.

During the 1980s, the most significant discoveries and new mines were made and developed in Nevada and the Hemlo district of Ontario, Canada. These and other new mines throughout North America were the result of higher prices, new technology, and the ease of raising funds for mine finance. The most important technological improvement was heap leaching which made possible and profitable the exploitation of many previously uneconomic low-grade ore bodies.

Heap leaching is a process used by the mining industry for the extraction of gold and other metals from ores. Crushed ore is piled into large mounds covering several acres and a liquid cyanide solution is continuously sprinkled on top of the heap using systems not much more sophisticated than lawn sprinklers. As the solution percolates through the ore, the gold is dissolved and later recovered from the collected solution. Often the ore is in surface deposits, allowing low-cost excavation of open pit mines.

Several factors contributed to the ease of fund raising for mining finance during the 1980s:

1. The high prices and still optimistic outlook for gold during the early years of the decade attracted capital to the industry.

2. The increasing disfavor of South Africa among many investors led to a shift of international investment funds from South Africa to other regions.

3. Tax incentives in Canada—principally the concept of flow-through shares which allowed investors to reap special tax benefits—helped finance much of the exploration and development in Canada during the past decade.

4. The availability for the first time of gold loans for mining finance. In a gold loan, the mining company borrows gold from a bank or bullion dealer at interest rates well below the cost of alternative debt finance, sells the gold for cash to pay for the development of a new mine, and eventually repays the loan in bullion out of its future production.

gold loan

Now, many of the heap leach mines that contributed to the rise in U.S. production are running out of minable reserves while output from the giant Hemlo deposit is also peaking. In addition, many of the factors

S. Africa is starting to attract Int'l capital once again.

which had earlier supported an expansion of gold mining across North America are no longer present. Lower prices and a bearish outlook have discouraged exploration and development by mining companies and have discouraged gold lending by bullion bankers; South African disinvestment has not only run its course, but that country is beginning to attract international capital once again; and Canadian tax incentives are no longer available.

Lower prices, the difficulty in raising finance capital, and the depletion of low-grade, open pit, heap leach mines are also limiting the prospects for gold output in Australia. In addition, gold production "down under" has also been influenced by changes in the tax environment for gold mining companies. Australian gold output reached an all-time high of 7.8 million ounces (243 tons) in 1990—but by 1991 production was already contracting.

The imposition of income taxes on the gold mining industry, which had previously enjoyed a tax-exempt status, beginning in 1991 has skewed the profile of annual output. Companies altered mining practices in the years prior to taxation, particularly by targeting high-grade deposits at the expense of mine life, in order to accelerate income into the pretax years.

In the next few years, the costs of these practices will be seen in terms of rapidly declining gold production. By 1995, Australian gold production likely will be down to no more than 4.5 million ounces (140 tons) per year.

Forward Sales and Gold Loans

Supply effect when the sale is booked—not when the gold is actually delivered in the future.

Gold supplies arising from forward sales and bullion loans by mining companies and national producers are indistinguishable in the marketplace from current mine production and other sources of supply. Beginning in the mid- to late 1980s, these activities became an important source of total supply. In 1988 and 1989, forward sales and gold loans contributed 15 million ounces (467 tons) and 10 million ounces (311 tons), respectively, each year. By 1991, their contribution was probably about 6.0 million ounces (187 tons).

Typically, when a mining company sells gold for future delivery, the purchaser—usually a bullion dealer—will borrow the same quantity of metal from a central bank or other lender and immediately sell this borrowed gold into the market. When the mine delivers the gold, the dealer will return the metal to the original lender. So the supply effect on the market and the metal's price is felt when the forward sale is booked, not when the gold is actually delivered in the future.

Forward Sales

[handwritten: The borrowed gold enters the market at the time the loan is monetized]

Similarly, when a mine borrows bullion to finance development or for other uses, it sells the metal into the market in order to convert the loan proceeds into spendable cash. The borrowed gold enters the market at the time the loan is monetized. In the future, when the loan is repaid out of mine production it is returned to the lender rather than being sold into the market.

The impact of forward sales and gold loans has been to accelerate the growth in supply—but the same ounce of gold cannot be sold twice. Much of the next few years' gold production has already had its impact on the market and the metal's price. *[handwritten: Effect on market = to accelerate the growth in supply ↵]*

What counts is the net supply entering the market as a consequence of these activities—that is net of deliveries against previous forward sales and net of repayments against earlier gold borrowings by mining companies. Even though the gross rate of forward sales has continued to increase in 1990 and 1991, for example, the deliveries of gold sold in prior periods has also been rising rapidly. Moreover, the repayment of past gold borrowings has also exceeded new gold loans by a wide margin—and this situation is likely to characterize the next few years.

Declining Production and Sales by the Former Soviet Union

Political, social, and economic prospects in Russia and other CIS republics have deteriorated rapidly in recent years—and this is having major implications for world gold markets. The breakdown in these countries' political, social, and economic fabric is already limiting their ability to continue mining and supplying its historical quantities of gold. *[handwritten: USSR sales]*

Based on information available at the time of writing, it is clear that Soviet gold sales were significantly higher during the late 1980s and early 1990s than anyone had previously imagined. This helps explain why the price of gold was under almost constant pressure during these years despite the continuing tightening in other sectors of supply and demand. However, the high rate of Russian and other CIS republic gold sales drew heavily on the country's official reserve holdings—and by late 1991 these bullion holdings were nearly spent. As a consequence, the rate of Soviet gold sales must fall off sharply in 1992 or 1993 at the latest.

During the past decade, Soviet gold mine production probably totaled some 8 million to 10 million ounces (250 to 310 tons) per year. But gold mining has hardly been immune from the many problems plaguing the economy during the past few years. Output has been constrained by labor difficulties, ethnic unrest, and the economic dislocations (such as fuel shortages) widely reported in the country's major gold producing regions. By 1991, gold mine output in the former Soviet Union may have fallen to 6 to 7 million ounces (160 to 180 tons).

However, not all domestic gold mine production is available for sale internationally. The domestic jewelry industry probably consumes about 1.3 million ounces (40 tons) per year and the electronics, telecommunication, and defense industries probably use another 643,000 ounces (20 tons) annually.

Given the documented increase in domestic gold demand, especially for jewelry—which is being purchased in Russia and other CIS republics as a hedge against inflation and political uncertainties—the difficulties in gold mine production, and, most importantly of all, the fact that the former Soviet Union has sold nearly all of its official reserve holdings of gold, these countries will be unable to maintain a high rate of gold sales during the years ahead—despite their pressing need for hard currency.

Other East Bloc Gold Sales

In addition to the former Soviet Union, North Korea and the People's Republic of China supply regular quantities of gold to the world market from domestic mine production. North Korea possibly mines as much as 700,000 to 900,000 ounces (25 to 28 tons) of gold each year. Chinese gold mine production is now likely on the order of three million ounces (93 tons) per year. These production estimates refer to only official, state-controlled mining activity. Small-scale prospecting and mining also is important in both countries—but much of this gold is bartered in black markets and is ultimately hoarded domestically.

Over the past 10 years, aggregate East bloc sales have ranged from a low of 3.1 million ounces (96 tons) in 1983—a year in which Soviet sales were probably close to zero—to a high of almost 20 million ounces in 1991. Reflecting trends in the former Soviet Union, overall East bloc sales are likely to fall toward the middle to lower end of this range in the years ahead.

Significant quantities of gold are also smuggled into the East bloc. For many years, the flow of gold into Mainland China from Hong Kong and elsewhere—gold carried in the form of *chuk kam* (solid gold) jewelry and small bars by expatriate Chinese visiting family and friends in China—has been well documented. Over the years, gold has also likely been smuggled into the Soviet Union and other Eastern European countries or stashed in

Table 3.2. East Bloc Gold Sales (million troy ounces)

	1981	1982	1983	1984	1985	1986
U.S.S.R	6.2	3.6	0.0	1.8	3.7	9.6
China	2.2	2.3	2.4	2.5	2.6	2.7
North Korea	0.6	0.6	0.7	0.7	0.8	0.5
Total	9.0	6.5	3.1	5.0	7.1	12.8
	1987	1988	1989	1990	1991	1992
U.S.S.R.	4.6	7.4	10.3	12.9	16.1	3.2
China	2.8	2.9	2.9	3.0	3.0	3.0
North Korea	0.5	0.6	0.6	0.6	0.6	0.6
Total	7.9	10.9	13.8	16.5	19.7	6.8

SOURCE: American Precious Metals Advisors. Totals may not add due to rounding.

Western bank vaults by government officials and businessmen traveling abroad. The statistics in Table 3.2, "East Bloc Gold Sales," do not net out bullion smuggled into these countries or acquired and held abroad by East bloc residents. Instead, this component of demand is included in the net private investment data (see Table 2.1).

Secondary Supply *(Price sensitive)*

The recovery of gold from old scrap—known as secondary supply to fundamental analysts—contributes another 7 million to 14 million ounces (218 to 435 tons) a year to total market supplies. The sources of old scrap are dishoarded jewelry and coins, junked electronics and telecommunications equipment, and literally from the old teeth pulled by your friendly dentist.

In some measure, old scrap is price sensitive— and the declining price trend of the late 1980s and early 1990s has discouraged dishoarding of old jewelry and the scrappage of other gold-containing items. Secondary supply is also a function of economic conditions—particularly in the Middle East, India, and other Asian markets.

In these regions, gold jewelry is a traditional savings medium and store of wealth—much like savings accounts to Americans. When times are tough, people cash in their savings by selling gold jewelry back to the market. This was seen, for example, in early 1991 when the economic and political dislocations associated with the Gulf War caused distress sales of gold jewelry by residents and refugees from the area.

Apart from brief intervals when difficult economic conditions may provoke dishoarding of old jewelry, scrap or secondary supply will tend toward the lower end of its historical range when prices are low. Only as a bull market takes hold will secondary supply begin rising in a sustainable fashion.

4
Fabrication Demand

Introduction

Total fabrication demand for gold—from jewelry manufacturers, industrial consumers, and for dental applications—totaled 72 million ounces (2239 tons) in 1990. The lion's share—nearly 64 million ounces (about 1984 tons)—was used to manufacture gold jewelry. In recent years, jewelry manufacturers alone have consumed every ounce of gold produced by mines around the world.* (See Table 4.1.)

The ancient roots of gold jewelry can be traced back to the Sumerian civilization which flourished around 3000 B.C. in the Tigris-Euphrates valley of what is now southern Iraq. Surely its natural beauty and its incorruptibility made the metal a symbol of power, wealth, and perhaps even godliness to the aristocracy of early civilizations. But its special physical properties also made gold special. Its is malleable—so much so that it could be hammered into paper-thin sheets. It is ductile—so that it can be drawn into hair-like wire of extraordinary fineness. And, of course, it is incorruptible—in the sense that it is immune to most chemical reactions and neither tarnishes nor rusts like other metals.

*In keeping with the generally accepted accounting framework, mine supply and fabrication demand statistics exclude production and consumption within the former Soviet Union and other East bloc countries.

Table 4.1. Fabrication Demand for Gold (million troy ounces)

	1986	1987	1988	1989	1990
Jewelry					
Industrial Nations	18.9	18.8	21.6	26.2	27.8
Developing Nations	18.2	19.7	27.1	34.1	36.1
Total Jewelry	37.1	38.5	48.7	60.2	63.8
Industrial					
Electronics	4.0	4.0	4.3	4.4	4.4
Dentistry	1.6	1.5	1.6	1.6	1.6
Other Industrial	1.8	1.8	1.9	2.0	2.0
Total Industrial	7.4	7.4	7.8	8.0	8.0
Total Fabrication	44.5	45.9	56.5	68.2	71.8

SOURCE: Gold Fields Mineral Services and American Precious Metals Advisors, Inc. Totals may not add due to rounding. This table may not be reproduced in whole or in part without express permission of APMA.

For millennia, gold and gold jewelry was by its very nature available only to the ruling elite. But in the past century, gold jewelry has become accessible to many and is today a mass market consumer good. The ever widening appeal of gold jewelry to more and more people around the world will be a major bullish facet of the market during the 1990s.

Indeed, growth in demand for gold jewelry already has been the most positive feature of the market during the late 1980s and early 1990s—and this will continue to be one of the more dynamic sectors of the market during the years ahead.

Two Types of Jewelry Demand

The nature of jewelry demand and the physical characteristics of the jewelry itself tend to vary between the major industrial nations on the one hand and the developing and newly industrial nations on the other.

Jewelry purchased in the United States, Western Europe, and Japan, for example, is bought as a luxury and fashion item for adornment and conspicuous consumption. The purity of the gold, itself, ranges from 8 karat (which is an alloy only 33 percent of which is fine gold) to 18 karat (containing 18/24 or 75 percent fine gold). The retail price of jewelry purchased in these countries carries a huge markup over the cost of the gold itself and is often a multiple—as much as 200 to 400 percent—of the value of the gold contained in the item.

KARAT is a measure of gold's purity or "fineness." The word originates from the ancient Greek word *karation* and the Arabic word *qirat* meaning fruit of the carob tree. Carob seeds were used in ancient markets as standard weights. 24-karat gold is pure gold of at least 0.999 fineness. 22-karat gold is 22 parts gold and 2 parts other metals; in other words, it is 22/24 pure gold or 0.9167 fine. 22-karat gold is favored for jewelry in many Middle Eastern and Asian markets. 18-karat gold is 18/24 pure or 0.750 fineness; this is the legal minimum purity in Italy and France for an item designated as gold. 14-karat gold is 14/24 pure or 0.583 fine. 14-karat gold is the popular purity of gold jewelry in the United States.

Jewelry demand in the industrial countries is very much a function of economic and business conditions. When times are good and income growth is strong, consumers buy more jewelry.

In contrast, in the developing and newly industrialized countries—for example in the Middle East and Asia—jewelry is purchased as much, if not more, as a means of saving or investment rather than simply an adornment and status symbol. And, the jewelry itself tends to be of higher purity, usually 21 to 23 karat (from 88 to 96 percent fine gold). Sometimes, jewelry may even be manufactured in 24-karat pure gold as in the case of *chuk kam* jewelry which is popular in Mainland China and Southeast Asia. In these countries, demand also responds to economic conditions—but it is also very responsive to the price of gold itself. At low prices, consumers and savers perceive a bargain and tend to buy more than at high prices.

Window on the U.S. Jewelry Market

Just how big is the gold jewelry market in the United States? According to the World Gold Council, the size of the primary value* gold jewelry market in this country was $8.5 billion in 1989—and more than 96 million individual gold jewelry items were sold. Many of these were relatively inexpensive items. The average price paid for a piece of gold jewelry was only $88, making gold jewelry accessible to a broad spectrum of Americans regardless of their income and wealth.

*This is jewelry in which the primary value lies in its gold content and excludes items where diamonds or other gems represent the piece's primary value; also excluded are gold watches.

The heaviest purchasers of gold jewelry are men and women between 25 and 54 years of age. Although this group account for only 53 percent of the adult population, they bought more than 70 percent of the gold jewelry sold. Consumers in households with incomes over $30,000 accounted for 62 percent of the items purchased and 68 percent of the dollars spent on gold jewelry. This also means that households with incomes of less than $30,000 accounted for 38 percent of the items purchased and 32 percent of the dollars spent on gold jewelry.

Not surprisingly, women's jewelry accounts for the bulk of the U.S. market. 84 percent of the units acquired and 76 percent of the dollars spent in 1989 were for items designated as women's jewelry. Interestingly, women are also becoming increasingly important purchasers of gold jewelry. They bought 66 percent of the items designated as women's jewelry, representing 58 percent of the dollar volume. Men's purchases on the other hand, accounted for only 34 percent of the volume and 42 percent of the value of women's gold jewelry purchases.

Compared to other types of fine jewelry, gold is available in a wide range of styles and price points—making gold jewelry attractive and affordable to a broad spectrum of the American population. Compared to more faddish merchandise categories, gold benefits from its high quality, durability, and long-term value.

Strong Growth in Jewelry Demand

Worldwide jewelry demand for gold has risen rapidly over the past decade—from 16.5 million ounces (514 tons) in 1980 to about 63.8 million ounces (1984 tons) in 1990 and roughly 66 million ounces (2053 tons) in 1991. This is equivalent to an average annual increase of more than 13 percent over the period. To be fair, jewelry consumption was depressed in 1980 by record high gold prices and an unfavorable economic climate. But in recent years, jewelry demand has continued on a rapid growth track—expanding by 27 percent in 1988, 23 percent in 1989, and more than 8 percent in 1990. The point is not how much jewelry demand grows in any one year but how much it is likely to expand over the 1990s—its long-term prospects.

A number of factors contributed to the rapid growth in worldwide gold jewelry demand over the past decade—and point to continued expansion in the years ahead:

1. Years of economic expansion in the major industrial nations have given jewelry buyers more disposable income and wealth than ever before. Even with a recession in North America and the United Kingdom in 1991, global economic growth has continued, albeit at a reduced rate, but sufficient to prompt some rise in jewelry demand. Even if the world economy continues along a sluggish growth track during the next few years, jewelry demand will continue rising from one year to the next.

2. Gold prices are at historically low levels, particularly in real or inflation-adjusted terms. Moreover, for consumers in many countries around the world, changes in exchange rates over the past decade have made local currency gold prices still more attractive. Low prices are an important spur to rising jewelry consumption in many of the developing and newly industrialized countries in the Middle East and Asia.

3. Demographic trends in the major gold jewelry consuming nations will continue to favor growth in jewelry demand as a larger proportion of the populations move into the age groups most likely to buy. Additionally, the growing proportion of working women—particularly in higher paying professions—is similarly benefiting jewelry demand.

4. Investor and savings related demand for high-karat, low-value-added gold jewelry continues to expand in many of the Asian and Middle Eastern markets. Further industrialization and improving business conditions in many of these countries means that their savings demand for gold jewelry will remain strong.

In many of these countries, gold has a long tradition spanning the generations as a reliable means of saving and preserving wealth. Even today, in some countries like India and Mainland China—both large population countries with rapid inflation and political uncertainties—there are no acceptable alternative savings institutions for a large majority of the people. Indeed, gold demand in these two countries—much of which takes the form of jewelry—is now on a path of rapid long-term expansion.

In addition, there is a continuing geographic dispersion of gold jewelry manufacturing and consumption and an expansion in the number of jewelry fabricating companies serving both local and export markets around the world. This expansion has been encouraged, in some countries, by government deregulation of local gold import and/or trading controls and, in other cases, by the improved economic and business climates which have fostered domestic jewelry demand. In particular, Thailand, Hong Kong, and Japan have emerged as important jewelry manufacturing centers in the Far East. In the Middle East and Asia Minor, Turkey is rapidly becoming an important manufacturer and Saudi Arabia is also enjoying a booming local business.

Spotlight on Asia (Japan & China)

Gold has cultural, historical, and social roots throughout the Far East. Gold has always been greatly treasured for its monetary aspects as a store of value and as a means of payment—but it is also an important symbol of prestige in societies where "face" is so important. Savings rates are high throughout Asia by world standards, reaching 20 to 30 percent among the more affluent in some countries. The populations of these countries have an affinity toward gold and a high propensity to buy gold jewelry, both as a store of wealth and as a luxury item and consumer good.

In 1990, Asia—including Japan and China but excluding India and Pakistan—accounted for 36 percent of the world's population, about 20 percent of world gross national product, and roughly 37 percent of global gold consumption, much of it in the form of jewelry. By the turn of the century, the region will account for 37 percent of the world's population, 27 percent of world gross national product, but probably 50 percent or more of total global gold consumption.

The economies of the so-called four little dragons—Hong Kong, Singapore, Taiwan, and South Korea—have grown by 7 to 8 percent in real terms over the past decade. During the 1990s, this group of rapidly growing Asian economies will be joined by Thailand, Malaysia, Indonesia, and possibly China. Reflecting these trends, Asia will be a growing consumer of gold over the coming years.

Other Industrial Uses

In addition to jewelry, gold is used in electronics, dentistry, and a variety of lesser industrial applications. It is gold's special physical properties which support its use by industry. In electronics, for example, the metal's high electrical conductivity, its resistance to corrosion or tarnishing at even extreme temperatures, and its ductility and workability have assured that no other metal can substitute for gold as a contact and conductor in everything from dishwashers to space shuttles. Worldwide gold use by the electronics industry now totals about 4.6 million ounces (143 tons) per year.

In dentistry, gold's corrosive resistance, malleability, and nontoxicity makes it ideal for various applications including crowns, bridges, and fillings, although often as an alloy with other metals. Dental use of gold now totals about 1.6 million ounces (51 tons) a year. Other industrial uses, especially as a decorative coating—for china, tablewear, bathroom fixtures, and personal items such as pens and other accessories—require about 2.0 million ounces (64 tons) per year.

Together these various industrial uses, excluding jewelry, consume a little over eight million ounces (about 250 tons) of gold each year. Over the years ahead, these uses are likely to grow a bit, reflecting growth in the world economy—but the changes (whether up or down) are not likely to be big enough to greatly alter the outlook for gold one way or the other.

Summing Up the Fundamentals

Table 4.2 presents prospective annual demand for gold from the world jewelry industry and from other industrial consumers. Annual jewelry demand through the end of this decade is projected on the basis of a very conservative 3 percent average annual rate of growth. This compares with actual growth of 13 percent per year from 1980 through 1991. Other industrial uses in total are projected to grow even more slowly—at just over 1 percent per year.

These are very conservative assumptions and are likely to be exceeded—but they illustrate the pivotal point of this book: The gold market will move from a small surplus position at the beginning of the decade to a small deficit, possibly as early as 1992, and a large deficit late in the decade unless prices rise sharply enough to alter the prospective evolution of supply and demand.

Table 4.2. Prospective Fabrication Demand for Gold (million troy ounces)

	1991	1992	1993	1994	1995	1996	1997	1998	1999
Jewelry	66.0	68.0	70.0	72.1	74.3	76.5	78.8	81.2	83.4
Industrial	7.9	8.0	8.1	8.2	8.3	8.3	8.4	8.5	8.6
Total Fabrication	73.9	76.0	78.1	80.3	82.6	84.8	87.2	89.7	92.0
Total Supply	90.8	75.0	75.0	75.0	75.0	75.0	75.0	75.0	75.0
Surplus or deficit	16.9	−1.0	−3.1	−5.3	−7.6	−9.8	−12.2	−14.7	−17.0

SOURCE: American Precious Metals Advisors, Inc. Totals may not add due to rounding. This table may not be reproduced in whole or in part without express permission of APMA.

5
Central Bank and Official Sector Demand

Despite the oft-quoted description of gold as a "barbarous relic," by John Maynard Keynes, the famous economist, central banks continue to hold the metal as sacrosanct. Official reserve holdings of gold by central banks and international monetary institutions have hardly changed in decades. In fact, over the past 40 years central bank gold reserves in absolute terms have actually risen by 12.5 percent. And, contrary to popular belief, the official sector was a net buyer of gold during the 1980s, adding 27.7 million ounces (862 tons) to their holdings over the decade. Today, reported official sector gold reserves total more than 1140 million troy ounces. Valued at $350 an ounce, these official stocks are worth about $400 billion—no trifling sum.

One important premise of this book is that if gold is good enough for central banks its good enough for the private individual and institutional investor. Apart from this, many of gold's naysayers fear that future central bank sales will depress the metal's price in year's ahead. In reviewing the place of central banks in the world of gold and the place of gold as a central bank asset, this chapter is intended to prove the former and disprove the later.

Official Sector Holdings

The official sector consists of central banks of individual countries as well as certain international institutions, namely the International Monetary Fund, the European Monetary Cooperation Fund, and the Bank for

International Settlements, each of which holds gold as part of their assets. In addition, certain national investment authorities (such as the Kuwaiti Investment Authority) may own some gold—but these are not counted as official gold reserves.

As can be seen in Table 5.1, although there has been a redistribution of

Table 5.1. Official Sector Gold Holdings
Historical Data (year-end totals, million troy ounces)

	1950	1960	1970	1980	1990	1991*
Industrial						
United States	652.0	508.7	316.3	264.3	261.9	262.0
Canada	16.6	25.3	22.6	21.0	14.8	14.1
Australia	2.6	4.2	6.8	7.9	7.9	7.9
Japan	0.2	7.1	15.2	24.2	24.2	24.2
Austria	0.2	8.4	20.4	21.1	20.4	20.4
Belgium*	16.8	33.4	42.0	34.2	30.2	30.2
Denmark*	0.9	3.1	1.8	1.6	1.7	1.7
France*	18.9	46.9	100.9	81.9	81.9	81.9
Germany*	n/a	84.9	113.7	95.2	95.2	95.2
Greece*	0.6	2.2	3.3	3.8	3.4	3.4
Italy*	7.3	63.0	82.5	66.7	66.7	66.7
Netherlands*	9.0	41.5	51.1	43.9	43.9	43.9
Norway	1.4	0.9	0.7	1.2	1.2	1.2
Portugal*	5.5	15.7	25.8	22.1	15.8	15.9
Spain*	3.2	5.1	14.2	14.6	15.6	15.6
Sweden	2.6	4.9	5.7	6.1	6.1	6.1
Switzerland	42.0	62.4	78.0	83.3	83.3	83.3
United Kingdom*	81.8	80.0	38.5	18.8	18.9	18.9
Other	1.7	3.0	1.9	1.9	2.8	2.8
Total industrial	863.6	1000.7	941.4	813.9	795.9	795.2
Oil exporting	20.8	20.3	33.5	40.6	43.2	43.7
Other developing	71.2	62.3	84.8	101.6	101.4	100.8
Total all countries	955.6	1083.3	1059.7	956.1	940.5	939.6
European Monetary Cooperation Fund	—	—	—	85.6	93.5	93.5
International Monetary Fund	42.7	69.6	124.0	103.4	103.4	103.4
Bank for International Settlements	1.5	−0.5	−8.1	7.5	7.8	7.3
Grand total	999.8	1152.4	1176.9	1152.6	1145.2	1143.8

SOURCES: International Monetary Fund and American Precious Metals Advisors. Totals may not add due to rounding.
*Excludes amounts transferred to European Cooperation Monetary Fund.

gold reserves among countries, the total amount of gold held by all countries has hardly changed in over four decades. Central banks hold onto their gold, generally preferring when pressed to expend foreign exchange reserves or borrow abroad rather than deplete their gold holdings.

(change 1997 ?.)

The Distribution of Gold Reserves

Among central banks, the big gold holders remain the major industrial countries of North America and Western Europe. At the end of 1990, the United States held 22.9 percent of total world gold reserves, Germany held 8.3 percent, Switzerland and the United Kingdom each held 7.3 percent, and France 7.2 percent. (See Table 5.2.)

The developing countries of Asia, the Middle East, and Africa together held only 12.6 percent of total world gold reserves at the end of 1990. In recent years, there has been a tendency of the newly industrialized nations—which are still counted in the developing nations category—to add to their gold reserves as their national wealth has grown. This trend may have important implications for the future.

Another positive trend has been the shift of gold reserves from individual countries to international agencies, particularly the European Monetary Cooperation Fund. This forerunner of a common European Community central bank requires member countries to contribute 20 percent of their gold holdings to the reserves of the fund. Gold held by international agencies like the European Monetary Cooperation Fund (EMCF) or the International Monetary Fund (IMF) is held under fairly restrictive conditions and is not likely to be sold. At the end of 1990, the three international monetary agencies—the IMF, the EMCF, and the Bank for International Settlements (BIS)—together held 204.7 million ounces of gold or 17.9 percent of total world gold reserves.

Unreported Gold Reserves

All of these statistics are based upon data reported to the International Monetary Fund by its member countries. So holdings by nonmembers are not included. Among the big omissions are Russia and the other CIP republics, who were not yet members at the time of printing. Little actual information has been available about the quantity of official gold reserves held by the former Soviet Union and other East bloc countries that had not been members of the IMF.

Table 5.2. Central Bank Gold Reserves as a Percent
of Total Reserves—Selected Countries
(year-end 1990 totals, million troy ounces)

	Total Gold Reserves	% of Total Reserves
Lebanon	9.22	84.3
Algeria	5.14	73.2
India	10.69	73.0
Pakistan	1.95	71.7
Uruguay	2.40	62.9
South Africa	4.09	61.0
Afghanistan	0.97	58.4
United States	261.91	58.3
Philippines	2.89	54.6
Switzerland	83.28	52.3
F?⅝?Netherlands*	43.94	49.2
Belgium*	30.23	48.8
Czechoslovakia	2.53	46.9
France*	81.85	46.1
Austria	20.39	45.6
Peru	2.21	45.0
Germany*	95.18	35.1
Venezuela	11.46	34.7
Portugal*	15.83	29.6
Italy*	66.68	29.0
Greece*	3.40	27.7
Argentina	4.37	26.6
Jordan	0.75	25.4
Canada	14.76	24.2
Turkey	4.09	20.2
Libya	3.60	19.2
Brazil	4.57	19.1
United Kingdom*	18.94	16.9
Australia	7.93	15.8
Mainland China	12.70	14.2
Indonesia	3.11	13.8
Saudi Arabia	4.60	13.2
Yugoslavia	1.91	11.8
Morocco	0.70	11.5
Sweden	6.07	11.5
Japan	24.23	10.6
Spain*	15.61	10.5
Finland	2.00	7.4
Thailand	2.48	6.7
Nigeria	0.69	6.4

Table 5.2 Central Bank Gold Reserves as a Percent
of Total Reserves—Selected Countries
(year-end 1990 totals, million troy ounces) (Continued)

	Total Gold Reserves	% of Total Reserves
United Arab Emirates	0.80	6.3
Denmark*	1.65	5.7
Columbia	0.63	5.4
Israel	0.84	4.9
Iceland	0.05	4.2
Poland	0.47	3.9
Mexico	0.92	3.5
Norway	1.18	2.9
Ireland*	0.36	2.6
South Korea	0.32	0.8
New Zealand	0.00	0.0
Luxembourg*	0.43	0.0

SOURCE: International Monetary Fund.
*Excludes amounts transferred to European Cooperation Monetary Fund.

By the time this book is published, the former Soviet republics will have most likely revealed the actual quantity of gold held in the past few years—and this total is probably much lower than most observers had believed until very recently. In addition, a number of other countries hold gold outside of their reported reserves—as an asset of a national investment authority, in a trading account, or simply because they prefer secrecy.

Gold as a Proportion of Official Reserves

Although the actual quantity of gold held by the official sector has changed little over the decades, the proportion of total official reserves represented by gold has been declining over the years. At the end of 1990, gold accounted for only 28.5 percent of total official reserves. A decade earlier, the ratio of gold to total reserves was about 58 percent. This decline reflects the change in the price of gold itself—from an excessively inflated level in 1980 to a depressed price level more recently—as well as the substantial growth in the foreign exchange reserves held by the official sector.

Theory :.. Absence of a significant rise in the metals price ... (central banks) are more apt to be buyers Rather than sellers.

With gold's proportionate importance declining, central banks today are more likely to feel underweighted in gold relative to their historical positions. This suggests that central banks, in the absence of a significant rise in the metal's price (which would inflate the value of gold reserves and increase their weight as a component of total reserves) are more apt to be buyers rather than sellers.

The only international asset NOT Representing a claim on someone else.

The Attributes of Gold

Why do central banks hold gold? Why are they apparently so reluctant to part with what they've got?

Perhaps they know something about the future that the rest of us don't. More likely, they hold gold because of their penchant for safety and security in managing their national assets. Gold is the only international asset not representing a claim on someone else. In other words, gold is not contingent upon any other country's or institution's discretion. In recent years, renegade countries—like Iran—have seen their international assets frozen, but gold bullion held in their own vaults offered safety and liquidity not found in other financial assets.

Most countries pursue diversification, trying to balance their portfolio of official assets in order to minimize a variety of possible risks. And gold has proven itself to be a great diversifier in a portfolio of various national currencies which typically comprise the balance of most countries' reserve holdings.

Gold ... great diversifier in a portfolio of various national currencies which typically comprise the balance of most countries' reserve holdings.

Other Central Bank Activities

Central banks do more than simply hold gold. Many trade, lend, or swap it to achieve various objectives. About 35 central banks are active today as lenders of gold, placing bullion on deposit with bullion bankers or dealers who will pay a small interest rate for gold deposits. Some central banks write covered calls against a portion of their gold holdings in order to generate income, and a handful of central banks have entered into gold swaps, using their gold as collateral to guarantee repayment of a loan. The former Soviet Union, for example, made use of its gold in this way, borrowing billions of dollars from Western banks at favorable interest rates.

On balance, the official sector can hardly be viewed as a threat to gold. The metal is too important to too many central banks for their to be any purposeful degradation of gold. Instead, central banks—as major gold holders—have a vested interest in stable or higher bullion prices.

Lenders of Gold

1997 – Change in Central Banks thinking – Australia (sold 60% holdings in 1997.

6
Investment Demand

Soviet Union borrowing against its gld.

" "Investors and speculators collectively were willing to add to their cumulative gold holdings only at progressively lower prices levels."

Introduction

The annual surplus of gold available in the market to satisfy private investment and speculative demand, as well as net central bank demand, has been shrinking from one year to the next since the late 1980s. Despite this improvement in the supply and demand fundamentals, gold remained under pressure through the early 1990s, in part, because investors and speculators collectively were willing to add to their cumulative gold holdings only at progressively lower price levels.

Investment obviously includes the demand for physical bars and bullion coins—that is, the actual purchase of the yellow metal by individual and institutional investors. However, many people participate in the gold market through other less direct channels than the outright purchase of bullion.

The activities of investors and speculators on gold futures, options, and other derivative markets also affects physical bullion demand through arcane arbitrage channels. For example, as investors and speculators buy gold futures contracts on a commodity exchange, the normal relationship between spot and futures prices will be affected. This creates an opportunity for large-scale dealers and arbitrageurs to profit by simultaneously selling gold for future delivery on the commodity exchange and buying the actual metal in the physical market. As a consequence, the behavior of investors and speculators in these other arenas often influences the metal's price just as if they were buying and selling directly in the physical market.

In addition, although strictly speaking not gold investment, per se—because the motives for purchasing and holding are somewhat different—demand for commemorative and nonbullion coins, medals, and medallions consumes a significant quantity of gold every year.

A New World for Gold Investment

Over the years, three interrelated trends—government deregulation, democratization, and globalization of the gold and gold investment market—have changed the gold world in a number of important ways. To begin with, the successive emergence of new geographic markets has been fostered by the legalization of gold ownership and the breakdown of regulatory impediments to gold investment and trading in one country after another.

For example, private gold ownership was legalized in the United States beginning at the start of 1975, Japan eased the restrictions on gold investment in the early 1980s, Brazil legalized private investment in the late 1980s and took steps to foster a local market, and a number of Asian countries—Taiwan and South Korea, for example—removed barriers to gold investment in the past few years. Today, all of these countries are significant players in the world of gold, and this has brought millions of new investors and potential investors into the gold world.

Though much of the importation of gold is through informal smuggling channels, the People's Republic of China has become a big consumer of gold as the Chinese seek ways to hedge against local inflation as well as political and economic uncertainties. And, in the early to mid-1990s, with the opening up of the former Soviet Union and Eastern Europe, the number of potential gold investors in these countries is also on the rise.

At the same time, the distribution channels for gold investment in many countries have moved from the coin shops, jewelry stores, and bazaars to the major financial service firms, mainly securities brokerage houses and banks. These firms have created new varieties of *paper gold* products—such as storage accounts and gold certificates—which have securitized gold and made the investment process far more efficient than it had been in earlier periods. In the United States, for example, firms such as Merrill Lynch, Shearson Lehman Brothers, and Bank of America make the purchase of gold as easy as investing in stocks, bonds, or bank accounts.

The entry of these financial service companies and the development of new products has helped legitimize gold investment and made it easier for more people around the world to participate if they so choose.

During a prolonged bear market the significance of these developments has not been well appreciated. However, once a new bull market commences and gold prices start moving higher again, more people in more countries will begin buying gold through a modern and sophisticated distribution system. This geographic expansion of the market and the improved access to gold investment is one important reason why I'm so bullish about the long-term prospects for gold. *Bullish !!*

East vs. West *(Asians & midEast) (BARgain Seekers & LATe Comers)*

Simplifying matters, there are two basic types of gold investors: what I call "bargain seekers" and "late comers." Bargain seekers—mostly Asian and Middle Eastern investors—like to buy gold when it is cheap in there own currencies. Because they step in and buy more gold whenever the price drops sharply, they have helped to limit downward price moves in the bear market of the late 1980s and early 1990s. But, these bargain seekers withdraw from the market when prices are rising—and, as a result, they are not likely to fuel a major bull market advance.

In contrast, late comers—mostly Americans and Europeans—tend to jump on the band wagon once prices are in a clearly defined uptrend. During bear markets, as prices fall, they become increasingly disinterested in gold and many dishoard metal that had been bought at higher price levels. While bargain seekers have helped to support a weak market, the behavior of late comers has accentuated the downtrend in the price of gold since the mid-1980s.

The Return on Gold

Since gold investors receive no interest* and no dividends, the only return on their holdings comes from price appreciation. When prices are rising this return is positive, but in a bear market the return on holding gold is negative.

Westerners implicitly calculate the expected rate of return on holding gold by projecting its recent past performance into the future. When gold

*Large institutional investors and central banks can receive interest by lending their bullion, but the opportunity to earn interest on gold is not available to the average investor.

performs well, these investors expect this trend to continue. But when gold does poorly, they become discouraged and demoralized about future prospects. This is the situation we find ourselves in at the start of the 1990s.

Since the mid-1980s, many Westerners gradually dishoarded gold as they lost interest in the market. But Easterners, attracted by lower prices, happily bought. As a result, during the past decade, there has been an almost invisible transfer of gold ownership from Western investors to Asian and Middle Eastern investors.

Significantly, late comers will add upward volatility to the gold price once the next bull market gets underway. In the future, these investors will return to the market—not necessarily because of higher inflation, financial crises, or world anxieties as many gold bugs predict—but because they are attracted by a gold price which is already rising on account of tightening fundamentals. As they return, the incremental investment demand will boost the metal's price still further and attract still stronger investment interest.

This time around, unlike prior bull market episodes for gold, investors collectively will find it difficult to satisfy their appetite for the metal. The market surplus is fast disappearing so that prices will quickly be bid higher as a growing number of investors around the world compete for a very limited quantity of gold. In fact, by 1992 or 1993, the market surplus is likely to disappear altogether to be replaced by a small deficit as illustrated by Table 4.2.

Moreover, the shift in ownership from West to East has put more of this metal into strong hands which are unlikely to dishoard even at very high price levels. This competition for scarce ounces of gold at a time of an unprecedented market deficit will push gold to new record high prices before the end of the decade.

Other Factors Affecting Gold Investment

Other factors may also influence the demand for gold among investors. We have all come to think of gold as an inflation hedge—and, at times, high or rising inflation has prompted interest in the yellow metal. Similarly, international political tensions, economic or financial market uncertainties, currency market turbulence, and investor perceptions about gold's own supply and demand fundamentals can also affect investor interest in the metal. (See Figs. 6.1, 6.2, and 6.3.)

Figure 6.1.

Price of Gold vs. CPI
1976 – 1991

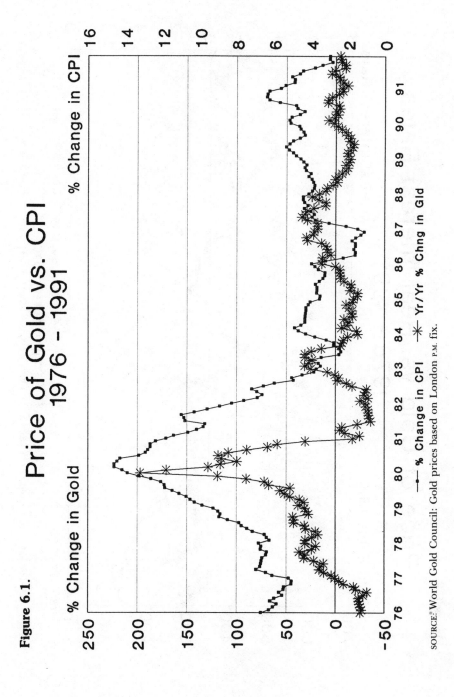

SOURCE: World Gold Council: Gold prices based on London P.M. fix.

59

Figure 6.2.

Price of Gold vs. Real Interest Rates
1976 – 1991

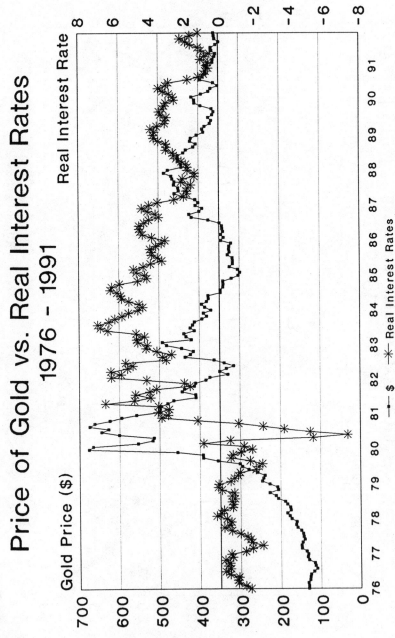

SOURCE: World Gold Council: Gold prices based on London P.M. fix; real interest rates equals the T-bill rate less CPI.

Figure 6.3.

Gold Price vs. Trade Weighted Dollar
1975 - 1991

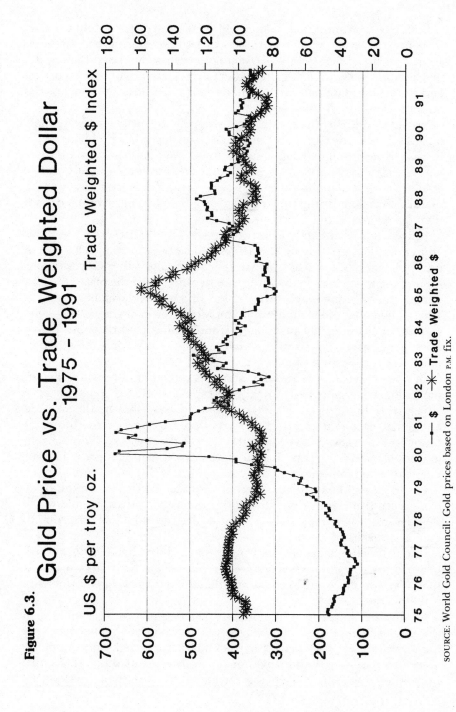

US $ per troy oz.

Trade Weighted $ Index

— ■ — $ —✳— Trade Weighted $

SOURCE: World Gold Council: Gold prices based on London P.M. fix.

61

But there is no automatic linkage which guarantees rising gold prices in response to developments in these other areas. During the 1970s, it seemed to many that gold was reacting to the rise in U.S. inflation, the depreciation in the dollar against other currencies, the surge in oil prices, and major international crises such as the Iranian hostage drama or the Soviet invasion of Afghanistan.

In contrast, during the 1980s and early 1990s the metal seemed to show little reaction to the sort of international crises and other problems which in earlier years might have resulted in a rising gold price. The stock market crash in October 1987 did, for a time, result in a slightly higher gold price—but even this response was fairly muted. More typical was the market's reaction during the Persian Gulf War. Gold briefly rallied—but then quickly retreated.

Just what differentiated these two periods—the 1970s versus the 1980s and early nineties? During the 1970s, gold prices were in a long-term uptrend—largely because the United States and other governments around the world had, in the four prior decades, fixed the price at $35 an ounce, and once the market was free to find its own level, beginning in 1968, it had a lot of catching up to do. Moreover, many investors—who had either been legally prohibited from owning gold or chose not to during the years of fixed prices—felt inclined to add some gold to their portfolios for the first time ever.

During these same years, the expected return on alternative investments looked unappealing: Real interest rates—that is, nominal rates adjusted for inflation—were low or even negative; stock markets looked questionable; and the U.S. dollar was depreciating against the major foreign currencies. As a result, the expected return on holding gold looked attractive to many investors versus the expected returns they might receive from these other assets.

In the 1970s, the dramatic jump in oil prices also transferred income and wealth from countries with a low propensity to invest in gold to the Middle East, where people had a historical and traditional attraction to gold as a means of savings.

But as the 1980s began, gold prices peaked and headed downward. This led to expectations—which were reinforced as the years wore on—that prices would continue to fall and that the returns on gold ownership would be negative.

Meanwhile, thanks to tight monetary policies and loose fiscal policies in the United States during the Reagan years, real interest rates were very high by historical standards, the stock market boomed, and the dollar looked increasingly sound. Investors logically concluded that the return on holding these other assets was far more attractive than the expected negative returns on gold. During these years, the dollar served as the safe haven asset in gold's stead at times of international crisis.

Now, in the early 1990s, the gold world is once again changing. Nominal and real interest rates are low once again, stock markets look wobbly, and many fear that the dollar is vulnerable. On the other hand, gold prices are depressed and many believe that they can't go much lower. In a sense, the situation today is opposite to that of the early 1980s. To many investors, the expected return on holding gold is starting to look attractive relative to the expected return on holding other conventional investment assets.

More importantly, as gold prices rise during the next few years, more and more investors will reassess the prospects for gold. As they look at the future through a rearview mirror, they will conclude that the prospective returns on gold ownership are attractive enough to warrant adding more of the metal to their collective portfolio.

PART 2

The Investment Vehicles

7
Bullion Coins

Introduction

Think of the typical investment pyramid—in my view, physical gold forms a solid cornerstone to the foundation. It's conservative, risk averse, and provides an insurance policy against many of the hazards associated with your other financial investments.

But what form of physical gold ownership is best? Investors can choose from a large menu of investment items: coins of various types and brands, small bars and wafers, larger bars, and a variety of paper proxies for gold including certificates, warrants, storage accounts, and some newfangled hybrid products.

For most investors, bullion coins are the ideal medium for gold ownership. Certainly, bullion coins are the best starting point for a new investor and should form the core of nearly every gold investment program. That's because bullion coins are not only the easiest and most convenient way to buy, hold, and resell gold but they are also the safest.

Bullion Coins Defined

Gold coinage has its roots at least as far back as the sixth century B.C.—but true legal tender bullion coins didn't appear on the scene until 1970, when South Africa first introduced its Krugerrand coin. For the first time, here was a coin that was bought and sold simply on the basis of its gold content value. Its price moved up and down in lockstep with the price of gold on the world bullion markets, hence the name *bullion* coin.

The closest things to gold investment coins prior to the introduction of the Krugerrand were *restrikes* that were issued by a number of different countries. The Austrian 100-Corona, the Mexican 50-Peso, and the British Sovereign were all low premium gold coins that were minted in numbers sufficient to satisfy any market demand. These restrikes were copies of earlier circulating gold coins, even bearing the date of the original issue rather than the actual mintage year.

In the past two decades, several countries—including Canada, the United States, Britain, Australia, and Austria—have followed South Africa's lead in issuing gold bullion coins. Since their introduction more than 20 years ago, investors around the world have bought over 65 million ounces of gold in the form of bullion coins.

The Advantages

Before the introduction of bullion coins, many investors bought either gold bars or numismatic coins. Neither were ideal for many investors. Bars are often too big and expensive for most people—and, for many, they are difficult to buy, resell, and store. On the other hand, numismatic coins—including older coins like the British Sovereign, French Napoleon, or old American Double Eagle as well as modern issue commemorative coins—are not pure gold investments. The price of numismatic coins reflects their scarcity, condition, and appeal to collectors, rather than their gold content. They often trade at substantial premiums, as much as several hundred percent above the value of the contained gold. In short, the price of a numismatic coin reflects its appeal as a collectible. Moreover, the market for numismatic coins is illiquid, so there are usually wide spreads between the price charged to an investor and the price received upon resale.

What makes bullion coins so attractive?

First, they are a pure gold investment. The price of a bullion coin fluctuates with the price of gold on world markets. Actually, 1-ounce bullion coins trade at a small premium—usually 5–8 percent at retail—above the "spot price" of gold quoted in the New York and London wholesale or interdealer markets. But the premium value is relatively stable and usually investors can recapture most of the premium they initially paid when they resell. Fractional coins—half-, quarter-, and

[handwritten note at top: Dealer pays 3% above spot price. "spread around $1 or $2 / oz.]

tenth-ounce sizes—usually carry a bigger premium and, while they may be attractive gift items, are not recommended for the serious investor.

Multiple-ounce bullion coins were introduced by the Australian minting authority, Goldcorp Australia, in 1991. These 2-ounce, 10-ounce, and kilogram (32.1507 ounces) coins trade at progressively lower premiums. However, I do not recommend these larger coins for most investors because they still lack liquidity and their market needs to pass the test of time.

The wholesale premium on the major 1-ounce bullion coins—that is the markup dealers pay when purchasing coins in bulk from national mints or in the interdealer market—is usually about 3 percent above the spot price of gold. Often, it will be this wholesale premium—rather than the retail premium paid by investors—which is reported in the newspapers.

Second, bullion coins are liquid. In other words, bullion coins are very easy to buy and, more importantly, they are easy to resell. Liquidity also assures a narrow bid-ask spread, so that what a retailer or broker quotes as his selling price to you is not much higher than the price at which he will repurchase the same coin. In recent years, this spread has often been around $1 or $2 for the popular 1-ounce coins. Liquidity is analogous to resaleability.

Third, they are easy to store, easy to transport, and internationally tradable. Bullion coins are not a hassle. They are fabricated in standard 1-ounce and fractional units that are within every investor's budgetary grasp. Thus, they offer investors a means of accumulating a long-term holding on a regular, affordable basis. And, like a good wine, a name brand coin will travel well around the globe, fetching the same price from one country to the next.

Fourth, they are difficult to counterfeit. The degree of fine detail, the precision measurements of both diameter and thickness, the color, and of course the weight, when taken together make it virtually impossible for a professional to be fooled by a fake coin. Retailers and dealers can readily verify a coin's authenticity. So as long as you're doing business with a reputable, experienced broker or retailer, the risk of purchasing less than you bargained for is negligible. Moreover, there is no costly assay requirement when bullion coins are resold.

Fifth, it's easy to figure out what your coins are worth. When the Krugerrand was first introduced in the 1970s, it caught on immediately in part because it contained precisely 1 troy ounce of gold. Previously, the popular gold coins (like the French Napoleon or the Austrian Corona) contained fractional amounts of gold that made calculating its value difficult. With a 1-ounce bullion coin, the value is always close to the current price of gold in world markets.

Important Choices

Today, as an investor, you can choose among a number of major bullion coin brands and you can buy from numerous retailers, banks, and brokers. Never have gold investors been so well served. Table 7.1 highlights the chief characteristics of the major coin brands. With all of these choices, what's an investor to do?

First and foremost, do business with a reputable dealer or broker. It is absolutely amazing how many sophisticated investors have fallen for precious metals scams and frauds. Choosing the right dealer is as vital for your financial health as the right doctor is for your physical health and well being.

Buying gold coins should not be part of a "get rich quick" scheme. Instead, they are the foundation of a conservative, prudent personal investment and wealth protection program. You should buy gold coins as much for protection—like life and fire insurance—as for appreciation, so why expose yourself to unnecessary risks by dealing with a retailer who doesn't measure up to the highest standards.

Moreover, it's so easy to buy coins from many securities firms, banks and thrift institutions, reputable and established coin dealers and shops, and even some insurance companies. You're probably already doing business with someone who can sell you coins—perhaps your stockbroker, bank, or insurance broker—so start there if you can. Make sure the company you deal with makes a two-way market and will repurchase the coins when you are ready to resell. But also shop around. Check the

Table 7.1. The Popular Bullion Coins

Coin	Issuing Country	Date Intro.	Fineness	Product Range
Krugerrand	South Africa	1970	0.9167	1 oz–$^1/_{10}$ ounce
Maple Leaf	Canada	1979	0.9999	1 oz–$^1/_{10}$ ounce
Panda	China	1982	0.999	1 oz–$^1/_{10}$ ounce
Eagle	United States	1986	0.9167	1 oz–$^1/_{10}$ ounce
Nugget*	Australia	1987	0.9999	1 oz–$^1/_{10}$ ounce
Britannia	United Kingdom	1987	0.9167	1 oz–$^1/_{10}$ ounce
Philharmonic	Austria	1989	0.9999	1 oz–$^1/_{10}$ ounce
50-Peso†	Mexico	n/a	0.900	1.2057 ounces
100-Corona†	Austria	n/a	0.900	0.9802 ounces
Sovereign†	United Kingdom	n/a	0.9167	0.24 ounce

*In 1991, Australia introduced gold coins in 2-ounce, 10-ounce, and kilogram (32.1507 ounces) weights.

†These coins are restrikes.

pricing—including the premium, any commissions, and the bid-ask spread—for both purchases and resales. Then pick a retailer or broker who is reputable as well as competitive.

Now which brand is best? Among the major coin brands, there is really not much difference from an investment perspective. But, I'd begin with one of the more popular brands that has already passed the test of time because chances are best that they will be more liquid, that is easier to resell at full value, in the future. In the United States, the American Eagle leads the market; in Europe, the Austrian Philharmonic is the best seller; and worldwide the Canadian Maple Leaf is number one. Either of these brands is fine. Moreover, for the top brands the going prices are listed in *The Wall Street Journal, Barron's,* and the financial pages of many other newspapers so its easy to keep tabs on your dealer's pricing.

Diversify Against Risk

At some point, it also makes sense to diversify you coin holdings among a few brands. Diversification reduces risk.

Some years ago, the South African Krugerrand was the most popular, most liquid, most internationally accepted gold bullion coin. Then, as one country after the next imposed economic sanctions prohibiting the importation of South African coins, the Krugerrand market was disrupted, resaleability diminished, the premium disappeared and for a time was replaced with a small discount. Some firms stopped dealing in Krugerrands and many investors stopped buying them, so their value declined to a point at which dealers and refiners could profitably purchase dishoarded coins, melt them down, and recast them into standard good delivery bars. This was at a discount of 2 or 3 percent below the wholesale world price of gold and as much as 10 percent below the resale price of an American Eagle or Canadian Maple Leaf.

The liquidity—in terms of resaleability, stability of premium, and narrowness of the bid-ask spread—depends on the issuer's commitment to servicing its market and dealer network. It's conceivable that the United States, Canada, or any other government that now issues gold bullion coins could retreat from this market in the future, ceasing the marketing and promotional support necessary to maintain its coin's liquidity. In addition, as the Krugerrand's demise illustrates, if the issuing country fails to pass some political litmus test its coin can suffer a loss of public acceptance.

In the worst of cases, your coins will always fetch close to their gold content value. At the very least, they will sell for their scrap or remelt value, a few percent below the wholesale price of gold. But the prudent investor will diversify against this risk by owning a portfolio consisting of several coin brands. In other words, don't put all of your golden eggs in one basket.

If you are fairly wealthy and have accumulated 50 or 100 ounces of gold bullion coins, split equally between American Eagles and Canadian Maple Leafs, it's time to consider some of the other major brands. Make sure you are buying a legal tender coin or an official restrike from a country which has a commitment to marketing its coin year after year. The Australian Nugget, the Mexican Peso, and the Chinese Panda are good choices. And the Austrian Philharmonic, while newer, also qualifies. This coin is the only 0.9999 fine European bullion coin—and since its introduction has been a big seller in its own country. While aesthetic appeal is one of the least important criteria for selecting a particular coin, the Philharmonic is a beautiful coin with an unusual musical motif which will appeal to many coin buyers.

Unless you're a bona fide collector and numismatist, don't buy earlier mintages of any of these coins that may have other than the standard 5 to 8 percent premium. In some years, the quantities minted were sufficiently small—the Chinese Panda, for example—that they have gained a scarcity value among collectors which is reflected in a larger price premium above its gold content value. The larger the premium, the less gold-like is your investment and the greater your risk to nongold influences.

Although all of the popular 1-ounce gold coins do contain 1 ounce of gold, some are alloyed with other metals to affect their hardness or color. If so, the coin will actually weigh more than 1 ounce, reflecting its nongold metallic content. The American Eagle and the South African Krugerrand, for example, are 91.67 percent pure—the equivalent of 22-karat gold—and 8.2 percent of their total weight is other alloying metals.

Some investors prefer coins like the Canadian Maple Leaf, Austrian Philharmonic, or Australian Nugget which are all 0.9999 fine—that is, pure 24-karat gold with no alloying metals. Arguably, these coins have less premium risk in the event of a disruption of their resale markets. That's because refining to remove alloying metals is not required in order to recast these coins into standard good delivery bars.

The old Krugerrand is also recommended if you can buy the coin from your retailer at close to its gold content value, that is without paying a premium. So many of these coins had been sold around the world prior to the imposition of import bans by the United States and many other countries that they are readily available in the secondary or resale market.

While some of the larger banks and dealers, succumbing to political pressures, stopped dealing in the South African coins years ago, many shops still carry them. Since you are paying little or no premium, the risk of premium erosion is not significant. In fact, now that South Africa has been accepted back into the world community, the Krugerrand premium could eventually return to par with other popular bullion coins.

Other Considerations

Sales (purchase) subject to state Sales Tax of Value added tax

Check whether the coin you are buying is subject to sales or value-added tax in your state, province, or country. Perhaps your country's own brand will be exempt or maybe you can make arrangements to buy elsewhere. Often this can be accomplished by phoning a broker or dealer in another locality.

Once you have bought your first coin, take good care of it. Make sure you store it in a safe deposit box at your bank and insure it against theft. Alternatively, keep your investment in a reputable and insured bullion depository.

Some investors purchase gold coins because they don't leave a paper trail. (Drug dealers and others of the underworld use gold coins for much the same reason.) Wealthy individuals have long used gold as a means of quietly distributing assets to their heirs. Unlike securities purchases and many other investments made in the United States, the dealer is not required to report your purchase to the government. So no one—not even Uncle Sam—knows you own gold. Dealers, however, are required to report your resale to the IRS.

Establishing a Coin Buying Program

If you've never bought gold, decide first how much you'd like to invest in bullion coins. Will this be your only form of gold ownership—or will you also be buying other forms of bullion or gold mining shares? Read Part 3 for guidance about how much is appropriate.

As I've noted above, shop around for a coin dealer. If you are buying more than one or two coins, this is especially important because you will want the best price and service possible. If you are fairly wealthy and have sizable investment assets, your first few purchases may be for 50, 100, or even thousands of ounces as you establish a golden anchor for your portfolio.

If your an average investor, with only a few thousand dollars earmarked for bullion coins its important to add to your holdings periodically—perhaps every quarter or even once a year—as your income, savings, and overall wealth permits. Coins are particularly well suited to a regular periodic purchase program. For example, buy 1, 5, or 10 coins every month or quarter depending on your means. If you do this regularly, your average purchase price will simply reflect the average price of gold over time.

In either case, if you have never done business with the retailer, keep your first and perhaps your second purchase on the small side until you have learned the mechanics and the dealer has earned your trust. Remember, to diversify your holdings among a few coin brands if you are buying large quantities.

Summary

Bullion coins are ideal for the conservative, risk-averse investor. They provide a safe medium for buying and holding gold. They are convenient for those who wish to take physical delivery—or walk out of the coin shop with gold in your pocket. Bullion coins are the most anonymous means of holding gold. And they are appropriate for the investor with a long-term time horizon. Bullion coins are also befitting gifts whether your giving one to mark a birthday or anniversary—or giving many as a means of distributing wealth anonymously to your family and heirs.

Among the things you need to consider are the:

■ *Premium*—the additional cost of the coin over the price of bullion itself.

■ *Spread*—the difference between the bid and ask price for the coin.

■ *Liquidity*—how popular and easily recognizable is the coin, and, therefore, how easy will it be to resell?

■ *Aesthetics*—if attractiveness is one of your priorities.

■ *Country of origin*—if this matters to you.

8
Bars and Storage Programs

Introduction

While bullion coins are a fine gold investment vehicle for most investors, a variety of innovative bullion investment products and proxies provide today's gold investor with a wide selection of products. And, of course, bullion bars in larger sizes may still be a good choice for the very wealthy large-scale investor.

Besides bars and wafers, the menu of physical gold investment products includes certificates, warehouse receipts, passbook and accumulation accounts, storage programs, collateralized bank finance, and other leveraged programs. What's just as important is that many of these products are available today through Wall Street brokerage houses and banks across the country. As an investor, you can now buy gold bullion as easily as you would stocks, bonds, or bank certificates of deposit.

If you're fairly wealthy and taking actual physical possession of your gold is important to you, kilobars or 100-ounce bars may be appropriate—but smaller bars carry bigger premiums and are not as easy to resell as bullion coins. For the small-scale, average investor, buying gold bullion for physical delivery is neither as economical nor as efficient as purchasing bullion coins or the various paper proxies which are available through many brokerage firms and banks. I see no reason, whatsoever, to buy small bars or wafers. The advantages of bullion coins are well covered in Chap. 7.

Buying Larger Bars

As with any investment, first make sure you are doing business with a reputable dealer. If you're not certain, go elsewhere. Since most Wall Street brokerage firms have departments providing gold investment services, you should speak to your stockbroker.

But also shop around. Compare commissions and pricing. If you're buying a 100-ounce bar, its price at any moment should be close to the COMEX spot price—so ask first what you will be charged for the bar, then ask what the current spot price is on COMEX. [The Commodity Exchange Inc. (COMEX) is the world's leading gold futures exchange in New York.] Make sure you understand what other commissions or fees may be charged for the transaction. And, by all means, do business only with a broker who will stand ready to repurchase the bar from you in the future.

As you can imagine, retailers of gold are in business to make a profit—so the price at which they sell bullion will always be a little bit higher than the price at which they will buy bullion from either their suppliers or from the investing public. The price at which a dealer will sell you gold (or any other investment) is called the *ask* or *offer*. The price at which the dealer will repurchase metal is called the *bid*. And the difference between the bid and ask prices—the dealer's profit margin—is referred to as the *spread*.

In choosing a company with which to do business—whether it be your local coin shop, your broker, your bank, or some other outlet—make sure that the retailer maintains a two-way market and stands ready to repurchase your investment at the going price. And, make sure that his spread is reasonable and competitive with other retailers.

Many dealers will base their buying and selling prices on a benchmark such as the current spot price on COMEX or the most recent London fixing price. If the current COMEX price were $400 an ounce, for example, your broker might be a willing seller of a 100-ounce bar at $406 an ounce and a willing buyer at $404 an ounce. In the vernacular of the trade, the broker would be quoting a $2 spread. Keep in mind, that many brokers will also charge a commission on each and every transaction. This is analogous to a service charge levied when you buy and again when you resell.

Bar Brands and Other Considerations

Like most products, gold too comes in different brands—that is, they are the products of different competing refining companies. To assure ease of resale, buy a bar which qualifies as COMEX *good delivery*, bearing the brand of a COMEX-approved refiner. (The public information department at COMEX will provide you with a list of good-delivery brands.) Each bar will be stamped with the name of the fabricating refiner as well as a serial number and its exact weight.

Buying a COMEX-deliverable bar has an additional advantage. Most likely, the bar can be resold to the broker or banker with whom you already do your gold business—and from whom you originally purchased your bullion. But if you own a COMEX-deliverable bar, you will also have the option of selling it by entering into a short position on the Commodity Exchange.

If you're buying a large bar, don't take physical delivery outside a major precious metals depository. Instruct your broker or dealer to deliver the bar to an account in your name at one of the major precious metals depository or warehouse institutions in New York City or Wilmington, Delaware, for example. In most cases, they are departments of leading banks. Your broker should be able to handle all the necessary paperwork to set up such an account—or you can call the precious metals depository directly and set up your own storage account in advance.

Many investors who purchase gold bullion or coins wish to take delivery of the metal and store it in their own safe deposit box or under the proverbial mattress. But remember, the contents of bank safe deposit boxes are not insured by either the bank or by the federal government. So whether the gold is in your private safe deposit box, under your mattress, or in a shoe box in the back of your closet (that's where a relative of mine used to keep his gold and silver bars and coins), make sure that you have arranged for insurance against theft. Often, it's possible to add a rider to your homeowners or household insurance.

If you do take delivery of gold bullion, keep in mind that once your metal leaves the depository, chances are you will have to pay assay charges when you wish to resell. However, as long as it remains in an acceptable depository or warehouse your gold can be resold without incurring this additional cost.

Inquire about insurance. All of the major depositories will insure their customer's holdings. Also make sure that you have bought an allocated bar—that is, a bar which is designated by its brand and serial number to belong to you.

Futures markets offer an alternative means for purchasing large quantities of gold in 100-ounce units. Generally, you may acquire a warehouse receipt by purchasing a long futures position on the Commodity Exchange and stand for delivery as the contract expires. Since COMEX gold contracts represent 100 ounces, you will acquire a good delivery bar (or 3 kilobars) in a COMEX-approved warehouse. More on the workings of COMEX will be found in Chap. 11—but a commodities broker at any of the major futures commission merchants—generally the same Wall Street houses with whom you conduct your other investment affairs—will be able to guide you through this very simple transaction. Not only is it easy to buy gold this way, but often the costs and commissions will be more attractive. Should you ever wish to take actual physical delivery of your bar or bars, this can be arranged easily with the depository.

Paper Gold

Brokerage firms, banks, bullion dealers, and retailers have developed a number of paper products which make gold investing easier and, at the same time, reduce the commissions, fees, and premiums paid by small-scale investors. Paper gold gives investors many of the benefits of gold bullion ownership without the hassle. Investors in these products need not be concerned with delivery, storage, sales tax, assays, or any of the other details that go with investing in physical gold.

By paper gold, I am referring to gold certificates, storage accounts, accumulation plans, and other similar vehicles which allow the small-scale retail investor the opportunity of buying physical gold without taking actual delivery. Generally, in these gold purchase programs the metal is held in the vendor's account at a major precious metals depository.

When you purchase paper gold, make sure the bank or broker is actually buying and holding bullion in a segregated account on behalf of its clients. In other words, make sure that there are particular gold bars allocated to and backing the paper gold instrument. In no case should you buy gold that is merely an unallocated liability of the bank or brokerage firm. Allocated gold is legally owned by the customers and is not at risk should the vendor itself suffer financial problems or bankruptcy. Also, satisfy yourself that the broker and/or the depository has adequate insurance against loss.

Over the years, a number of companies have purported to sell paper gold products to their customers—but were later found out to have defrauded investors by never purchasing bullion on their behalf. One gold retailing company some years ago showed customers a vault piled high with bullion bars. Impressive? Perhaps, but investigators later found stacks of wood blocks coated with gold-colored paint. The moral is simple: Paper gold may be worth no more than the integrity of the seller—so make sure you know who you are dealing with. It's probably best to stick to one of the nationally known investment firms or banks who's names are household words.

Gold Certificates

One of the oldest forms of paper gold, certificates, were first issued by a number of banks, not only to provide a convenient means of buying gold, but to avoid the sales tax which might apply to physical delivery in some countries or localities.

Typically, a certificate attests to ownership of a specified amount of gold, often a specific bar, held on behalf of the investor at a particular gold depository. As a result, certificates are usually available in denominations corresponding to the sizes of standard bars. Sometimes, certificate programs provide a facility for delivery of the gold to the owner upon demand. If you think this may be important to you in the future, make sure the program you are considering offers this feature.

Storage Accounts and Accumulation Plans

Many brokerage firms offer storage accounts rather than certificate programs. Metal purchased and held in storage accounts will usually be commingled with the gold holdings of other storage account investors. The advantage is that it allows investment in fractional units (often hundredths or thousandths of an ounce) corresponding to a given dollar amount. For example, a customer investing $5000 at a time when the price of gold is $350 might have 14.286 ounces credited to his account.

As with any paper gold product, make sure that the gold is purchased and held by the broker or dealer at a reputable depository on behalf of its storage account customers. In some programs, there may be a facility allowing for physical delivery—but generally additional fees will be charged should you ask for delivery.

Accumulation accounts offered by brokerage firms and banks are a variant of storage programs. Accumulation plans provide a mechanism for the periodic (usually monthly) purchase of a fixed dollar amount of gold much like a payroll savings or withholding plan that allows employees to save or to buy company stock. You agree in advance to spend a certain fixed amount every month—and your broker or banker will automatically invest this money in gold on the same day, month in and month out. You should receive a regular statement indicating the total quantity of gold that you own and your average purchase price.

Accumulation plans serve as a convenient way to *dollar average* your purchases. By investing a fixed dollar amount, you will actually be buying more ounces of gold when the price is low and fewer ounces when prices are high. Accumulation plans are a good method for the risk-averse mainstream investor to acquire a physical gold position over a period of time because it takes the guesswork and speculation out of buying bullion.

Bank Financed and Leveraged Gold

Government regulations prohibit stock brokerage firms from selling physical gold on margin. You can, of course, use the gold futures market if you wish to achieve the leveraging benefits of margin. Although definitionally different, the concept of margin on futures exchanges is somewhat different (as explained in Chaps. 11, "Speculating in Gold Futures," and 16, the glossary) the result is the same: You get the benefits—and risks—of owning a large amount of gold while paying only a fraction of its full purchase price.

In a collateralized or bank financed gold purchase program, the vendor—a gold retailer, broker, or the bank itself—will arrange a loan for you with a bank for up to 75 or 80 percent of the value of your gold purchase. So, in effect, you will pay only 20 or 25 percent of the purchase price up front. Retailers who promote these programs will often advertise that you can "control" $5000 worth of bullion for only $1000 down or $100,000 in gold for only $20,000 down.

The lending bank, however, will hold your gold as collateral against your debt. If the price of gold falls sharply, the bank will likely require additional cash collateral or advance repayment of some portion of the loan so that the collateral value is never less than your outstanding debt. Failure to meet requests for additional margin will probably result in the sale of your gold by the lending bank. As with any loan, you will be required to make periodic interest payments; in addition, most banks will charge fees for storage and insurance.

A bank financed gold purchase program is similar to buying stock on margin—except the lender is a bank rather than the brokerage firm or other vendor. As with stock purchased on margin, you actually own the gold and pay a finance charge for the loan. In contrast, if you enter into a futures market contract to purchase gold, you don't actually own the gold represented by the long side of the futures contract—you own the right to buy the gold in the future at a predetermined price. In a futures market transaction, you don't have periodic finance and storage charges—but you are paying a premium for future delivery which, in theory, is related to the cost of financing and storing the underlying metal over the life of the contract.

Leverage contracts are another variation of the same theme, allowing acquisition of gold for a fraction of its current market value. As with a bank financed purchase—but unlike a futures contract—you will actually own the underlying gold. The contract is a legal obligation on the part of the vendor to make delivery of a fixed amount of gold in the future at a price determined at the time of purchase. Typically, the investor will be required to deposit 20 or 25 percent of the value of the gold at the time of purchase. Finance charges will be due periodically on the balance and you will be required to pay additional margin if the price of gold falls or risk having your position sold by the leverage firm.

While leverage contracts may appear to be an attractive gold investment vehicle for aggressive investors, many of the firms specializing in these contracts over the years have been less than reputable. You can achieve the same results using a bank financed program or the futures market without exposing yourself to the risks of an underregulated sector of the market. If you must deal with one of these firms, first make sure its reputable, make sure that your gold will be held in a segregated account and not commingled with the leverage firm's own assets, and make sure the seller maintains a two-way market, standing ready to repurchase your bullion at fair market value.

Summary

Gold investors today have a large menu of bullion products from which to choose in addition to coins. Large bullion bars may be economical and efficient investment vehicles for the wealthy individual or institution which is making a large-scale purchase. For the average investor, however, bullion coins or a range of paper gold products are the best choice.

As an average investor, if you must take delivery it's probably best to stick with the major bullion coin brands. But if you are content to leave your metal with the bank or brokerage firm with which you do business, then decide what type of program—certificate, storage, or accumulation—you feel most comfortable with.

As with any investment, its important to know the company you are doing business with. But if you are leaving your bullion in their safe keeping, you best be doubly sure it is safe and secure.

9
Investing in Gold Mining Shares

*

In the stock market crash of 1987:

1) Gold bullion retained its value

2) Gold mining shares perform much like other equities.   Leverage = gold Equities

3) A small change in the metals' price can result in a big change in gold equities prices.

Introduction

Gold mining equities are an excellent vehicle for participating in the coming boom in gold. But gold mining shares are not gold and they will not function as a bullion substitute in a well diversified portfolio. Remember the stock market crash of 1987. Gold bullion retained its value but gold mining shares performed much like other equities, losing value in tandem with the overall stock market. So before you buy mining shares, I'd advise at least a small position in the real thing—gold bullion or gold coins—as a portfolio diversifier and insurance policy against stock market and other financial risks.

Gold mining shares do provide leverage to changes in the gold price—so a small change in the metal's price can result in a big change in gold equity prices. Leverage works in both directions, however, and declining bullion prices can take a big bite out of your gold stock portfolio. Choosing the right stocks can minimize the risks over the longer term—and that's what this chapter is all about: choosing the right gold mining stocks.

How Much Is Right?

Investors often ask: How much should I invest in gold and gold mining stocks? In Chap. 7 I talked about the appropriate proportion of gold bullion or coins as a diversifier and insurance policy against certain portfolio risks. But what about mining shares?

One rule of thumb provides guidance for all investors. How much of your equity holdings would you invest in any one industry group when you're bullish on that sector of the economy? That's the same proportion that you should invest in a portfolio of mining stocks (or a gold-oriented mutual fund if you would rather let a professional do your stock picking) when your bullish on gold.

In other words, if you're a stock market investor how much of your total equity holdings would you be willing to put into computer stocks or health care stocks, for example, when you are bullish on these industry groups? If you answer 10 percent, that's how much you should feel comfortable committing to gold stocks when you're bullish on gold. If you're comfortable with a higher percentage for other industry sectors, that proportion should be a guideline suitable to you as a gold stock investor.

Why Investors Buy Gold Stocks

As equity investors, gold stock investors are participating in a share of the profits of a company from which they expect to benefit from capital appreciation and/or dividend payments. In other words, you expect that the company can produce gold at a profit—and, if you're bullish on gold, you expect that profit will rise substantially in the future. In addition, you may believe that a particular company will register good growth in the number of ounces produced annually or that it has a good chance of discovering new ore bodies and hence developing new mines.

Caveat Emptor

Mark Twain must have seen many an investor swindled by gold mining promoters. He concluded, "A gold mine is a hole in the ground with a liar standing next to it." Had he lived today, Twain might have thought differently. Here in North America there are a number of reputable, well run gold mining companies that are managed by highly professional and ethical executives, much like those found in many other industries. This chapter is about investing in those companies along with other well managed gold producing companies with headquarters or operations in Australia, South Africa, and even the United Kingdom.

This chapter is not about investing in nonproducing gold mines, penny stocks, and other speculations. It may be fine to speculate in a developing gold mine or exploration company—but that is not the same thing as investing in a gold producing company of some substance. In the former, you're betting that your company will strike it rich with a big discovery. In the latter, you're investing in the outlook for gold as well as in the management and resources of a given company.

At the end of this chapter, I'll offer a brief list of the more popular North American gold mining companies. Although I'm not making any specific recommendations, this list will provide a good starting point as you begin to investigate the gold equity investment opportunities available to you.

Beware of the Risks

Even if you're investing in established gold producing companies there are a number of risks that you need to be aware of as a prudent investor:

Most obviously, as with all gold investments, there is price risk. This is simply the risk that the price of gold will fall, pulling down with it the prices of gold equities.

Management risk is a function of the quality of the mine management, its team of executives as well as its board of directors. These are the people who are entrusted with your investment. Are they good at there jobs? That's an important question—but one that is often hard to answer.

If you are investing in a company with headquarters and/or operations outside the United States, you must also be concerned with country risk. Are changes in the legal and regulatory environment likely to be hostile to foreign investors? Are there other political risks? Could the mining operations be nationalized by the current or some future government? Mines in some countries may be negatively affected by social unrest or terrorist activities.

Foreign operations are also subject to exchange rate risk associated with a change in the countries currency value or convertibility. If you're investing in foreign companies, you must be concerned that future earnings and dividends can be paid to nonresident investors.

Unlike most other companies, gold mines are also subject to geological and metallurgical risks. Geological risks have to do with the consistency,

Replaceability of Reserves

reliability, and replaceability of the ore reserves. Metallurgical risks have to do with the ability to extract gold from complex ores.

For most investors, a sensible way to minimize these risks is to concentrate your holdings in the major North American gold mining companies. If you're aware of the additional risks and feel comfortable with them, some portion of your gold share portfolio may also be invested in South African and Australian shares. More savvy and sophisticated investors may be able to play differences in country valuations to their advantage.

Sensitivity to the Gold Price— *Leverage* Understanding Leverage

Gold mining equities generally offer leveraged exposure to changes in the price of gold itself. A small percentage change in the metal's price will result in a big change in share prices. For individual companies, leverage will be affected most by the mine's operating costs as well as the proportion of future production that has been presold (or hedged) at fixed prices.

A brief hypothetical illustration shows why mining companies are leveraged investments: Goldminco (an imaginary company) has a mine that produces 100,000 ounces per year at a production cost of $275 an ounce. Assume a current market price of gold of $375 an ounce. Annual earnings (before depreciation and interest costs) are $100 an ounce or $10,000,000. Six months pass and the gold price has rallied to $425 an ounce—a 13 percent increase. However, earnings are now $150 an ounce or $15,000,000—a 50 percent increase. Goldminco's share price would likely rise sharply—with the exact percentage gain also reflecting the market's expectations about the future gold price as well as the mine's life, the company's exploration potential, and other company-specific factors.

Some companies have intentionally reduced their exposure to gold price changes by preselling some proportion at fixed prices. This is prudent management for many mines because it minimizes the risks of a bear market and may guarantee the company's profitability in even the most hostile gold price environments. Obviously, companies with little or no forward sales have the most leverage to future changes in the metal's price. A bull market in gold would have a bigger impact on earnings for these companies than for others which have presold or otherwise hedged a sizable proportion of future production.

Cos with little or no forward sales have the most leverage to future changes in the metals price: Example:

Companies with little or NO forward sales have the most leverage to future (earnings) changes in the metals price.

Operating Costs, Ore Reserves, and Grade

Unless you are a sophisticated investment professional, chances are you will have to rely on Wall Street analysts, newsletter writers, and the investor relations departments of the companies themselves for much of the information and analysis you'll need in order to make educated investments. Here are some of the things you will need to know and understand.

One of the first things professional gold stock analysts look at is operating costs. Some companies produce gold for less than $200 an ounce; others are operating at a loss with production costs above the current market price of gold. Make sure you know the breakeven cost of production for each mining company under consideration.

Investing in a low-cost producer is a conservative approach. But a high-cost mine can offer substantially more leverage because the percentage rise in earnings will be much greater as the market price of gold advances.

Remember, however, that a low-cost unhedged mine (that is with no presold production) may offer more leverage than a high-cost mine that has sold forward the bulk of its future production for the next few years.

Operating costs will generally be determined by the depth of the deposit, the hardness of the rock, the amount of waste material that must be removed to mine the gold-bearing ore, the metallurgy and grade of the ore and the degree of difficulty in extracting the gold, labor costs, environmental regulations, location and accessibility of the mine, and so on.

After the cost of production, the next thing you should look at is the company's ore reserves. Ore is merely rock from which a mining company can profitably extract gold. Ore reserves are the amount of gold-containing rock on the mine property.

Reserves are designated as *proven, probable,* or *possible* depending on the amount of drilling and sampling that has been done by the mine geologists. Securities regulators and accounting professionals have stringent rules governing the designation of reserves. To be proven, drilling and sampling of ore must be closely spaced. Since this is an expensive process, many mines don't prove up more than a few years of future production. As a result, the quantity of proven reserves will not be a good indicator of the true mine life. Probable reserves are less rigorously defined while possible reserves are just that, possible but hardly assured.

Still, mining analysts and company officials should be able to offer an *unofficial* view about the mine's reserves and life. Mine life is merely total

Amount of gold contained in a Ton of rock
Mine life = Total Reserves (est)
94 divided by anticipated annual   The Investment Vehicles
production.

reserves (which may be estimated) divided by anticipated annual production.

Next, you will want to know something about the ore grade—that is the amount of gold contained in a ton of rock. Grade is generally reported in terms of ounces or grams per ton. Ore grades for underground mines must not be compared with ore grades for open pit (surface) heap leach mines. The former require very high grades to be economical producers while the latter can be profitable with extremely low grades.

Analyzing It All

In reviewing the reports of securities analysts and newsletter writers or in questioning the companies' investor relations departments, there are a number of indicators to look for and ask about.

First of all, the *earnings* forecast: What will the earnings per share be for the next one, two, or three years based on a conservative estimate of the gold price? Most analysts will estimate earnings at gold prices close to current levels. (If you're comparing estimates for different companies, make sure the gold-price assumptions are consistent. These estimates will account for expected production over the forecast horizon, projected production costs, and the amount of gold presold or otherwise hedged.

Second, the *price-to-earnings* ratio or P/E: This is a measure of the current share price relative to past or projected annual earnings per share. This ratio provides a simplistic means of comparing relative value—but it can also be misleading. Many of the higher quality, longer life mines with good year to year growth in earnings and production trade at higher P/Es, not because they are overvalued but because they are worth more. It's best to compare P/Es for similar companies in terms of annual production, cost structure, reserves, and location.

Many analysts believe that *cash flow multiples* are a better indicator of value. Cash flow adjusts for any writedowns which may distort earnings as well as depreciation. (In recent years, many mines have written off unprofitable operations and this has depressed earnings without actually affecting cash flow. Depreciation is the bookkeeping charge to account for capital investment in prior years.) The cash flow multiple is annual earnings plus any writedowns, noncash charges against earnings, and depreciation (all on a per share basis) divided by the share price.

In looking at ore reserves, *market capitalization per ounce of gold reserves* is a useful comparison of relative value. This will tell you how much you are paying for every ounce of proven and probable gold in the ground. ("Market capitalization" is merely the number of shares outstanding times the current share price.)

Payback period : Measure

Another measure of relative value is _market capitalization per ounce of annual production_. This is an indicator of what the market is paying for each ounce of current production. Comparisons can be misleading, however, because no account is made for mine life, costs, and other variables.

One of the handiest indicators, in my view, is the _payback period_. This is the number of years it will take the mining company—at today's gold price and likely production rates—to earn its current share price. This may be calculated as the market capitalization per ounce of current (and anticipated) annual gold production divided by the difference between the current gold price and the operating cost per ounce.

One thing that these analytical measures won't tell you is which companies will benefit from new discoveries or acquisitions that may fuel future corporate growth. Neither will they tell you much about the quality of management and how it is valued in the marketplace.

Investment Strategies

For most investors, the most prudent investment policy is to hold a diversified portfolio of high-quality, growth-oriented mining stocks. When you do your research look for companies that have a track record of good growth in annual ounces of production—and which are expected to continue growing in future years. These companies can be respectable performers even in a static gold price environment.

The more aggressive, savvy investor may benefit from rotation. An understanding of each company's likely relative performance at each point in the gold price cycle can be used to the investor's advantage. As you await a clearly definable cyclical upturn in the price of gold, it is best to concentrate your holdings in the major, well managed, most widely held gold mining companies.

The stocks of these companies are the first ones investors will turn to when gold starts to move up—so their share prices may be most responsive at the outset of a major gold price rally or new bull market. At the same time, generally they are often the most resistant to a downturn in the price of gold—so they are good defensive holdings if the bullion price reverses.

As the gold price continues to advance and the bull market seems more assured, aggressive investors may begin switching into the second-tier, mid-sized, higher-cost producers. The stock prices of these companies may have lagged early in gold's cyclical upturn—but, at some point, they should begin to outperform the majors.

Later in the cycle, the excitement will begin to percolate down to the

3/

smaller, third-tier companies. And, for speculators, this would be the time
to buy the penny stocks and exploration plays. Don't buy these stocks on
the expectation that they will hit pay dirt. Instead, hold them for a quick
gain as speculative fever overtakes reason in the gold and gold equity
markets.

4/

It may soon be time to switch back to the highest-quality, lowest-cost
producers because of their defensive nature—or sell your gold stocks
altogether and avoid the inevitable downturn. Near cyclical turning
points, wise investors know its better to give up the last opportunity to
gain than suffer the loses that will accompany a new bear market.

Major North American Producers

The core of a prudent, well balanced gold share portfolio will be a
number of soundly managed companies with good prospects for growth
in production in future years, relatively low operating costs, comfortable
balance sheets without excessive debt, and long reserve lives. Tables 9.1
through 9.6 present some of the salient statistics on the leading gold

Table 9.1. Selected North American Gold Producers
Annual Output (thousands troy ounces)

| Company Name | Annual Gold Output | | |
	1990	1991	1992
Amax Gold	355	330	350
American Barrick	596	700	1,200
Battle Mountain	340	420	400
Bond International Gold	592	560	675
Cambior	239	322	325
International Corona	734	685	605
Echo Bay	817	750	725
FMC Gold	332	320	320
Hemlo Gold	435	460	440
Homestake	1,175	1,200	1,200
LAC Minerals	785	845	845
Newmont Gold	1,680	1,540	1,600
Pegasus Gold	333	333	390
Placer Dome	1,411	1,540	1,650
Teck	500	450	420

SOURCE: American Precious Metals Advisors, and various mining companies.

Table 9.2. Selected North American Gold Producers
Comparative Statistics

Company Name	Market Capital ($ mil.)*	P/E Ratio†	Cash Cost ($/oz)†	Mine Life (years)*
Amax Gold		690	25	215
13				
American Barrick	3,290	19	200	21
Battle Mountain	640	49	235	20
Bond International Gold	610	n/a	280	11
Cambior	220	14	285	11
International Corona	1,080	29	235	14
Echo Bay	1,160			13
FMC Gold	345	44	220	9
Hemlo Gold	830	28	160	16
Homestake	1,390	n/a	270	14
LAC Minerals	1,310	41	255	11
Newmont Gold	3,645	29	215	18
Pegasus Gold	380	33	255	9
Placer Dome	2,700	35	245	18
Teck	1,550	24	170	18

SOURCE: American Precious Metals Advisors and various mining companies.
*1991 date
†1992 estimate

Table 9.3. Selected Australian Gold Producers
Annual Output (thousands troy ounces)

Company Name	Annual Gold Output		
	1990	1991	1992
Delta Gold	49	107	77
Dominion Mining	342	393	400
GMK	326	370	390
Highlands Gold	n/a	228	320
Homestake Australia	332	325	325
Kidston	337	190	155
Newcrest Mining	n/a	695	755
Placer Pacific	687	795	780
Sons of Gwalia	77	110	90

SOURCE: American Precious Metals Advisors, and various mining companies.

mining companies in North America, Australia, and South Africa. While the analysis of U.S. and Canadian producers may hardly differ, when investing abroad—especially in countries like South Africa and Australia—different political, economic, environmental, and tax situations may greatly affect the investment prospects of individual companies. In addition, exchange rate considerations may come into play.

For those investors wishing to concentrate their gold stock selections closer to home, here are nine prominent and popular producers from which to choose. Company fundamentals are always changing, so make sure your analysis is current and up to date. For this reason, my list does not imply any recommendation to invest—that's a decision which is left up to the reader/investor.

American Barrick

New York Stock Exchange symbol: ABX

Head office: 24 Hazelton Avenue, Toronto, Ontario, Canada M5R 2E2.

Since it entered the gold mining business in 1983, American Barrick Resources Corp. has become one of the premier gold producers in the world today. The company has interests in six producing mines. Output totaled 596,000 ounces in 1990. However, production could reach 1.3 million ounces in 1992.

Table 9.4. Selected Australian Gold Producers
Comparative Statistics

Company Name	Market Capital ($ mil.)*	P/E Ratio†	Cash Cost ($/oz)†	Mine Life (years)*
Delta Gold	90	9	200	8
Dominion Mining	210	10	310	8
GMK	475	18	270	13
Highlands Gold	485	11	90	14
Homestake Australia	320	19	280	13
Kidston	130	31	240	6
Newcrest Mining	945	18	275	14
Placer Pacific	1,105	27	190	14
Sons of Gwalia	100	6	255	3

SOURCE: American Precious Metals Advisors and various mining companies.
*1991 date
†1992 estimate

(handwritten note in top right margin: methods used.)

Its principal asset is the Goldstrike Mine in Nevada's Carlin Trend which was acquired in 1986 and now has reserves totaling well over 18 million ounces. Production from this one mine could exceed one million ounces in 1992 and should continue rising for the next five years. Roughly half of 1991 Goldstrike production is from heap leaching operations.

American Barrick has a healthy balance sheet. Average operating costs were $218 an ounce in 1990 and were close to $200 an ounce in 1991. Cash flow and earning per share are expected to grow rapidly over the next few years. Much of the company's production for the next few years is already sold forward or otherwise hedged. As a result, American Barrick's earnings are less vulnerable to a slide in the gold price than those of most other companies. *But less leverage, too.*

(handwritten note in right margin: Heap leaching)

Battle Mountain

NYSE symbol: BMG

Head office: 333 Clay Street, Houston, TX 77002

Production at Battle Mountain's Fortitude mine in Nevada will wind down in 1993 when most of the current reserves will have been exhausted. The company has interests in five other operating mines, one of which should expand output sharply in 1992 and two are at advanced stages of development and may begin production in 1993/1994. Battle Mountain also owns 56.5 percent of Nuigini Mining, which in turn has a 20 percent interest in the giant Lihir project in Papua New Guinea.

Battle Mountain produced close to 420,000 ounces at an average cash cost of about $192 an ounce in 1991. Production will probably be maintained at close to this level during the next few years. In 1991, the company started hedging its future production and intends to hedge up to 25 percent of its expected output.

Echo Bay Mines

American Stock Exchange symbol: ECO

Head office: 10180 101st Street, Edmonton, Alberta, Canada T5J 3S4

Echo Bay is a large North American gold producer with well established operations at its Lupin Mine in Canada's Northwest Territory and at the Round Mountain and McCoy-Cove projects in Nevada. Echo Bay is the operator of the 50 percent owned Round Mountain open pit mine,

Table 9.5. Selected South African Gold Producers
Annual Output (thousands troy ounces)

Company Name	Annual Gold Output		
	1990	1991	1992
Beatrix	353	350	350
Buffelsfontein	538	470	435
Deelkraal	308	295	300
Doornfontein	260	240	215
Driefontein	1,674	1,805	1,860
Elandsrand	455	485	530
Ergo	377	365	335
Freegold	3,602	3,710	3,700
Harmony	953	770	820
Hartebeestfontein	1,018	945	915
Kinross	395	385	380
Kloof	830	930	1,215
Libanon	236	260	255
Saint Helena	336	295	295
South Vaal	644	665	720
Unisel	179	155	165
Vaal Reefs	1,693	1,710	1,710
Venterspost	192	165	155
Western Deeps	1,238	1,325	1,325
Winkelhaak	408	360	355

SOURCE: American Precious Metals Advisors, and various mining companies.

the world's largest heap leach mine. Production in 1992 should total around 800,000 ounces, close to the 1991 level.

The company's future prospects depend greatly on its two Alaska projects, the Alaska-Juneau (in which it holds an 85 percent interest) and Kensington (50 percent interest). The A-J is planned to be a large underground mine with output of about 365,000 ounces a year at a cost of $225 an ounce. At both of these projects, further planning is still required and production is unlikely for several years.

The company engages in forward sales and other hedging techniques to improve the prices realized on its gold and silver biproduct sales. Unfortunately, the company cannot generate sufficient cash flow to accelerate its debt reduction and internally finance new developments and is, hence, dependent on a rising gold price for improving fortunes. Nevertheless, Echo Bay should offer good share-price leverage to a rising gold price and it remains a favorite of many investors.

Figure 9.1.

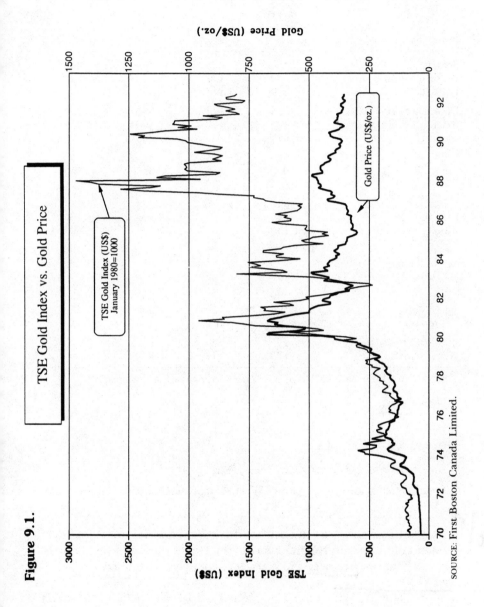

TSE Gold Index *vs.* Gold Price

SOURCE: First Boston Canada Limited.

101

Table 9.6. Selected South African Gold Producers
Comparative Statistics

Company Name	Market Capital ($ mil.)*	P/E Ratio†	Cash Cost ($/oz)†	Mine Life (years)*
Beatrix	480	23	260	20
Buffelsfontein	130	n/a	360	20
Deelkraal	220	n/a	310	23
Doornfontein	35	n/a	355	10
Driefontein	2,425	19	195	45
Elandsrand	615	26	255	45
Ergo	125	14	285	10
Freegold	900	13	324	15
Harmony	75	32	365	11
Hartebeestfontein	640	16	285	17
Kinross	245	15	275	16
Kloof	1,130	38	220	40
Libanon	30	n/a	380	10
Saint Helena	75	83	355	20
South Vaal	640	22	270	25
Unisel	80	265	355	17
Vaal Reefs	1,195	20	300	25
Venterspost	28	n/a	400	13
Western Deeps	915	29	275	30
Winkelhaak	175	n/a	305	20

SOURCE: American Precious Metals Advisors and various mining companies.
*1991 data
†1992 estimate

Hemlo Gold Mines

American Stock Exchange symbol: HEM

Head office: Commerce Court West, Toronto, Ontario, Canada M5L 1B6

Hemlo owns and operates one of the largest and lowest cost underground gold mines in North America, the Golden Giant Mine in northwestern Ontario. Just over 450,000 ounces per year are mined at a cost of only $130 an ounce.

With a 54.6 percent interest, Hemlo's principal shareholder is Noranda Inc. In mid-1990, Hemlo received all of Noranda's gold-related properties in exchange for shares. These assets include the small Silidor mine

Figure 9.2.

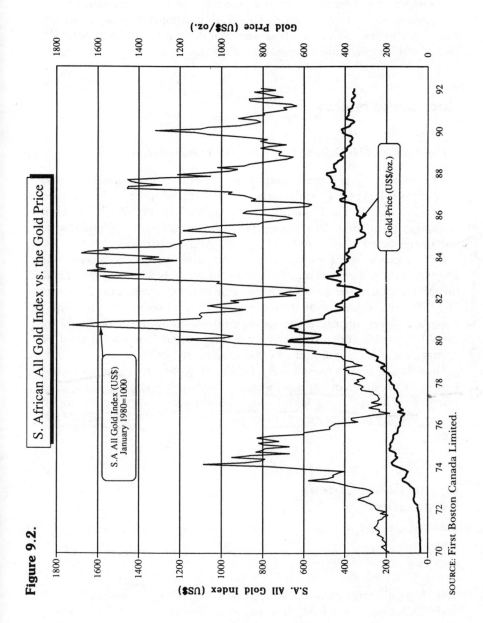

S. African All Gold Index vs. the Gold Price

S.A All Gold Index (US$)
January 1980=1000

Gold Price (US$/oz.)

SOURCE: First Boston Canada Limited.

103

in Quebec and three fairly well advanced exploration/development prospects which offer the company the possibility of future growth.

Hemlo has an extremely strong financial standing, reflecting its attractive earnings and cash flow, the absence of debt (aside from minor gold loan commitments) and a substantial cash position.

Homestake Mining

NYSE symbol: HM

Head office: 650 California Street, San Francisco, CA 94108

The company's principal asset is the venerable Homestake Mine in Lead, South Dakota. The property was first staked in 1876, Homestake itself was formed in 1877, and it has been listed on the New York Stock Exchange since 1889. As a consequence of its long history, Homestake is one of the best known, most widely held gold companies.

Its two major assets are the Homestake Mine, which produces about 360,000 ounces a year at an average cost of roughly $320 an ounce, and the McLauglin mine in California, with annual production of about 250,000 ounces at a cost of approximately $235 an ounce. In addition, it holds a 25 percent interest in the Round Mountain mine operated by Echo Bay and it controls the 81.7 percent owned Homestake Gold of Australia which contributed 282,000 ounces in 1990.

Homestake is a conservatively managed company which does not hedge. As a result, it offers maximum exposure to any changes in the gold price. This factor, along with its well known name among gold stocks, means that its share price will offer good leverage in a bull market for gold.

International Corona
Corporation

ASE symbol: ICRA

Head office: 120 Adelaide Street West, Toronto, Ontario, Canada M5H 1T1

With production running at approximately 725,000 ounces in 1991 and 605,000 ounces in 1992, International Corona is one of North America's biggest gold producers. Operating cash costs are less than $200 an ounce. The company's two main assets are its 50 percent interests in the

Figure 9.3.

Australian Gold Index vs. the Gold Price

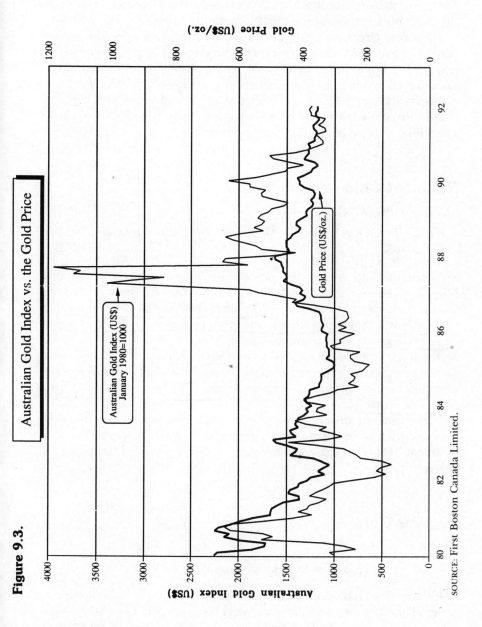

SOURCE: First Boston Canada Limited.

105

David Bell and Williams mines in the low-cost Hemlo district of Ontario. These two projects account for almost two-thirds of Corona's output. In all, the company has interests in 12 operating mines.

The Eskay Creek prospect in northern British Columbia is the company's hope for the future. Reserves on the property probably total well in excess of 3 million ounces of gold and 110 million ounces of silver. Commercial production is not expected until 1994 or 1995.

Despite its debt position, the company's financial situation is manageable. International Corona is an active hedger and typically sells forward a substantial portion of its next year's production.

Newmont Gold

NYSE symbol: NGC

Head office: One United Bank Center, 1700 Lincoln Street, Denver, CO 80203

Newmont Gold is the 90.1 percent owned subsidiary of Newmont Mining. (Newmont Mining, in turn, is controlled by the international financier, Sir James Goldsmith.) The company is the largest producer of gold in North America with 1990 output of nearly 1.7 million ounces. Cash production costs amounted to an average of $218 an ounce. Reserves at the end of 1990 totaled some 18.9 million ounces and its inventory of reserves are expected to grow from year to year as a consequence of its exploration program along its 38-mile long holding in the Carlin Trend of Nevada.

Under the control of Sir James Goldsmith, the company has embarked on a program of more aggressive exploration, expansion, and cost containment. It also has ceased all hedging in order to maximize exposure to the gold price.

Pegasus Gold

ASE symbol: PGU

Head office: N. 9 Post Street, Spokane, WA 99201

Pegasus Gold has made a specialty out of heap leaching and operates some of the largest and most successful heap leach mines in the world. The company's four mines produced 332,600 ounces in 1990 at an operating cost of $235 an ounce. The Zortman-Landusky open pit heap leach mine is one of the lowest-grade mining operations.

Pegasus has interests in a number of gold prospects including an option to a 50 percent interest in the Quartz Mountain project in Oregon and a joint venture with Lac Minerals to develop the Ortiz project in New Mexico. These—and the expansion of its Zortman mine with a planned start up in 1993—offer the possibility of growth in reserves and production over the next few years.

The company has been innovative in its financing and utilizes a variety of forward sales and hedging instruments.

Placer Dome

NYSE symbol: PDG

Head office: PO Box 49330 Bentall Postal Station, 1055 Dunsmuir Street, Vancouver, British Columbia, Canada V7X 1P1

Placer Dome is a major multinational mining company with important operations in Canada, the United States, Australia, Papua New Guinea, and Chile. Total attributable production is running about 1.5 million ounces per year from its 17 operating gold mines. Its newly commissioned Porgera mine in Papua New Guinea was projected to produce over 900,000 ounces in 1991 and over one million ounces in 1992. During the first half of 1991 cash costs at Porgera averaged about $65 an ounce. Overall, the company had cash operating costs averaging about $240 an ounce in 1991. The company also has significant production of copper and mlybdenum.

Declining ore reserves in recent years has forced Placer to aggressively seek new mines. In addition to its big developments in Papua New Guinea, the company is developing its 50 percent owned La Coipa gold-silver mine in Chile which is expected to produce 2.2 million ounces of gold and 114 million ounces of silver over its 13-year life at a gold cash cost of $178 an ounce.

Placer Dome has a strong financial position with plenty of cash to finance development of its various prospects and for future acquisitions. Although the company has utilized gold and silver loans for project finance, it has otherwise been a fairly conservative hedger, retaining a good degree of exposure to the gold price.

10
Gold Oriented Mutual Funds

Introduction

Mutual funds are touted as the right investment for the common man. When it comes to gold, however, gold oriented mutual funds may be right for some people some of the time—but they are not right for all investors all of the time. And, gold funds, like gold equities, are not a substitute for gold bullion.

Gold oriented mutual funds may satisfy the needs of many investors who want to hold a diversified portfolio of gold mining stocks. In addition to diversification, most offer the advantages of professional management—but not every gold fund is well managed. Moreover, not every gold fund gives the investor as much exposure to gold mining equities as might be expected. And, as discussed in Chap. 9, gold mining equities may not always perform like gold itself.

Be Aware of the Risks Before Investing

So, in electing to invest in gold mutual funds and in selecting the right fund, you need to consider the risks. Gold equities—and the mutual funds that invest in them—have some added risks including stock market risks and institutional risks.

Table 10.1. Gold Oriented Mutual Funds—Investment Fees. *n*,
Total Net Assets (Millions of Dollars)

Fund Name	12/88	12/89	12/90	12/91
Benham Gold Equity Index	7.5	61.8	101.6	124.0
Blanchard Precious Metals	20.1	34.7	30.0	25.2
Bull & Bear Gold Investors	42.4	46.6	34.4	28.1
Colonial Advanced Strategies Gold	84.0	82.5	53.5	38.3
Dean Witter Precious Metals	—	—	7.4	11.5
Enterprise: Precious Metals	3.2	6.0	6.2	4.9
Excel Midas Gold Shares & Bullions	12.8	11.2	7.6	6.2
Fidelity Select American Gold	191.5	259.8	206.6	148.3
Fidelity Select Precious Metals	199.9	253.0	189.2	145.7
Financial Portfolio: Gold	31.6	54.4	42.8	35.4
Franklin Gold Fund	259.1	327.2	289.0	257.2
Freedom Gold & Government	72.3	70.7	65.0	57.2
IDS Precious Metals	104.1	102.0	75.1	58.6
Kemper Gold Fund	4.0	6.9	12.0	—
Keystone Precious Metals	214.7	217.5	152.8	131.6
Lexington Goldfund	93.0	155.4	106.3	96.4
Mainstay: Gold & Metals	6.3	8.2	7.3	7.4
MFS Lifetime Gold & Natural Resources	1.9	4.7	8.0	7.0
Monitrend: Gold Fund	1.8	2.4	2.0	1.9
Oppenheimer Gold & Special Minerals	105.0	164.0	156.4	135.8
Pioneer Growth: Gold Shares	—	—	2.0	2.0
Rushmore: Precious Metals Index	—	1.5	4.9	9.0
Scudder Gold Fund	4.4	22.2	29.8	22.4
Shearson Investment: Precious Metals	91.2	92.0	59.9	41.5
Shearson Precious Metals & Minerals	43.4	34.6	23.4	17.2
Strategic Gold/Minerals	3.1	2.2	1.8	1.3
Strategic Investments	44.5	59.4	31.9	23.8
Strategic Silver	24.9	23.7	14.1	11.0
Sun-America: Precious Metals	2.0	3.2	3.0	1.1
Thomson: Precious Metals; A	—	—	—	0.6
Thomson: Precious Metals; B	—	9.6	8.5	8.3
United Gold & Government	99.6	83.3	54.5	40.7
U.S. Gold Shares	222.6	379.0	262.5	213.4
U.S. World Gold	96.3	98.5	68.5	57.1
USAA Investment Trust: Gold	176.3	177.9	141.1	118.7
Van Eck: Gold/Resources	228.6	252.9	175.0	136.3
Van Eck: International Investors	712.1	924.1	611.4	568.9
Vanguard Special: Gold	124.2	191.6	156.0	170.4
Total of 38 Funds	3328.4	4224.7	3201.5	2764.4

SOURCE: Lipper Analytical Services, American Precious Metals Advisors, and various fund companies.

MARKET RISK

These perils were aptly illustrated during the brief stock market crash of October 1987. Gold equities and gold funds crashed along with the market. When investors sold stocks, they sold everything including their gold mining stocks—pulling the prices of gold stocks down even though gold bullion retained its value.

Institutional risks were also evident. As the equity market was plummeting, some investors found their gold mutual funds to be illiquid because they couldn't get their fund companies on the phone. There just weren't enough lines to handle the volume of calls.

Then, too, there is management risk. Is the gold fund you've selected well managed by an experienced and qualified management team. Some gold funds have one portfolio manager. This person may lack the training and wealth of experience necessary to do the best possible job. In a few cases, he may even be a part-time gold fund manager, spending a significant share of his working hours managing another or several unrelated mutual funds. Or the manager may even be unscrupulous. Some years ago, one gold fund manager actually broke the law by investing a large part of his fund's assets in a couple of questionable penny stocks.

I've begun this chapter highlighting the risks because most investors think mutual funds are so safe they don't have to think. But, with a little forethought, gold oriented mutual funds can be a good vehicle for many investors to play the coming bull market in gold.

Commonsense Guidelines

Here are some commonsense guidelines for the gold fund investor:

1. Remember, just like gold mining equities, gold oriented mutual funds are not a substitute for a golden nest egg. One key theme of this book is that every investor needs to own some physical gold, be it coins or bullion, and even gold mutual funds which in turn invest a portion of their assets in bullion are no substitute.

2. Choose a well managed fund. This isn't as hard as it seems if you look for a management team (geologist, securities analyst, portfolio manager, gold stock trader) rather than an individual manager. And, at the very least, make sure the team or individual has been at his job for a number of years. Van Eck Management, which runs International Investors (the oldest and largest of the gold funds) and the Gold/Resources Fund, is one of the more experienced and most qualified management teams in this business.

But there are others too. For years, Harbor Capital Management has been doing a fine job running the Keystone Precious Metals Fund. The larger fund management groups don't have specialized management teams, but Fidelity and Vanguard both have good managers in charge of their gold funds. And, there are others, if you look carefully.

3. Make sure the fund you choose has a history of investing nearly all of its holdings in gold-related assets. This may include not only gold mining stocks—but gold bullion, gold-indexed debt, and even other precious metals. Some gold mutual funds, however, have the flexibility to invest a significant portion of their portfolio in cash equivilants (like Treasury bills, bank certificates of deposit, or commericial paper), unrelated mining or natural resource stocks and/or U.S. government debt.

One so-called gold fund has, in recent years, held nearly all of its assets in government securities, offering its investors little exposure to gold. When the bull market arrives, don't get caught short because your fund manager didn't see it coming and held something besides gold in your gold fund.

I'm not here to tell you everything you need to know about mutual fund investing. There are plenty of good books on the subject. Some will tell you to invest only in no-load funds—funds which have no upfront sales charge. Others will tell you to watch out for 12b-1 plans which allow managers to take an annual marketing fee out of the fund's assets. Some will warn about redemption fees.

The maximum sales and marketing fees for each gold fund are summarized in Table 10.2. Loads are a onetime, up-front sales charge, all or most of which may go to the stock broker who sells the fund. Loads often decline as the dollar amount of your investment increases. The 12b-1 fee is an annual charge levied against the fund by the management company to reimburse its marketing costs; some funds may charge less than the top authorized fee, but have the freedom to boost its charge to the maximum without shareholder approval. Finally, some funds collect a redemption fee when shareholders sell their fund shares and cash out. These redemption fees generally decline each year you remain invested in the fund, eventually falling to zero. It's best to check with the individual fund representative so that you understand what fees you may be charged.

But more important than all of this is to choose the right gold fund. In the long run, that's what counts the most.

Table 10.2. Gold Oriented Mutual Funds—Investment Fees

Fund Name	Load	12b-1	Redemption
Benham Gold Equity Index	None	None	None
Blanchard Precious Metals	None	0.75	None
Bull & Bear Gold Investors	None	1.00	None
Colonial Advanced Strategies Gold	5.75	0.25	None
Dean Witter Precious Metals	None	1.00	5.00
Enterprise: Precious Metals	4.75	0.45	None
Equitec Siebel: Precious Metals	None	1.00	5.00
Excel Midas Gold Shares & Bullions	4.50	0.25	None
Fidelity Select American Gold	3.00	None	1.00
Fidelity Select Precious Metals	3.00	None	1.00
Financial Portfolio: Gold	None	None	None
Franklin Gold Fund	4.00	None	None
Freedom Gold & Government	None	0.75	3.00
IDS Precious Metals	5.00	0.16	None
International Investors	8.50	None	None
Kemper Gold Fund	5.75	0.50	None
Keystone Precious Metals	None	1.25	4.00
Lexington Goldfund	None	None	None
M-S Mainstay: Gold & Metals	None	1.00	5.00
MFS Lifetime Gold & Precious Metals	None	1.00	6.00
Monitrend: Gold Fund	3.50	1.00	None
Oppenheimer Gold & Special Minerals	None	5.75	None
Pioneer Growth: Gold Shares	5.75	0.25	None
Rushmore: Precious Metals Index	None	None	None
Scudder Gold Fund	None	None	None
Shearson Investment: Precious Metals	None	1.00	5.00
Shearson Precious Metals & Minerals	5.00	None	None
Strategic Gold/Minerals	8.50	None	None
Strategic Investments	8.50	None	None
Strategic Silver	8.50	None	None
Thomson: Precious Metals; A	4.75	0.25	None
Thomson: Precious Metals; B	None	0.99	5.00
United Gold & Government	8.50	None	None
U.S. Gold Shares	None	None	None
U.S. World Gold	None	None	None
USAA Investment Trust: Gold	None	None	None
Van Eck Gold/Resources	6.75	0.25	None
Vanguard Special: Gold	None	None	None

SOURCE: *Barron's* Mutual Fund Quarterly, American Precious Metals Advisors, and various fund companies.

Table 10.3. Gold Oriented Mutual Funds—Telephone Numbers

Fund Name	800	In State
Benham Gold Equity Index	472-3389	800-321-8321
Blanchard Precious Metals	922-7771	212-779-7979
Bull & Bear Gold Investors	847-4200	212-363-1100
Colonial Advanced Strategies Gold	426-3750	None
Dean Witter Precious Metals	869-3863	None
Enterprise: Precious Metals	432-4320	404-396-8118
Equitec Siebel: Precious Metals	869-8007	None
Excel Midas Gold Shares & Bullions	333-9235	619-485-9400
Fidelity Select American Gold	544-8888	None
Fidelity Select Precious Metals	544-8888	None
Financial Portfolio: Gold	525-8085	303-779-1233
Franklin Gold Fund	342-5236	415-570-3000
Freedom Gold & Government	225-6258	None
IDS Precious Metals	328-8300	612-372-3733
International Investors	221-2220	212-687-5201
Kemper Gold Fund	621-1148	None
Keystone Precious Metals	343-2898	None
Lexington Goldfund	526-0056	None
M-S Mainstay: Gold & Metals	522-4202	None
MFS Lifetime Gold & Precious Metals	225-2606	617-954-5000
Monitrend: Gold Fund	251-1970	615-298-1000
Oppenheimer Gold & Special Minerals	525-7048	None
Pioneer Growth: Gold Shares	225-6292	617-742-7825
Rushmore: Precious Metals Index	343-3355	301-657-1500
Scudder Gold Fund	225-2470	None
Shearson Investment: Precious Metals	None	212-464-8068
Shearson Precious Metals & Minerals	None	212-464-8068
Strategic Gold/Minerals	527-5027	None
Strategic Investments	527-5027	None
Strategic Silver	527-5027	None
Thomson: Precious Metals; A	628-1237	212-482-5984
Thomson: Precious Metals; B	628-1237	212-482-5984
United Gold & Government	366-5465	None
U.S. Gold Shares	873-8637	None
U.S. World Gold	873-8637	None
USAA Investment Trust: Gold	531-8181	512-498-4499
Van Eck Gold/Resources	221-2220	212-687-5200
Vanguard Special: Gold	662-7447	None

SOURCE: *Barron's*, American Precious Metals Advisors, and various fund companies.

Country Considerations

In the early days of gold fund investing, fund managers put most of their money into South African stocks. Back in the 1970s and early 1980s, these South African mining companies were attractive because they were low-cost producers paying extremely high dividend yields—and, in large measure, they were the only game in town. North America and Australia had not yet developed major gold mining industries.

By the mid-1980s, gold mining companies were springing up in the United States, Canada, and Australia. At the same time, its apartheid policies were turning South Africa into an international pariah—and many gold funds began switching out of South African shares. More recently, these political issues have dissipated. But, reflecting rising costs and decreasing profitability, many of the South African mining shares are no longer attractive.

Today, the savvy gold fund manager may select a few South African stocks, just as he may choose to own a few Australian stocks. However, most of the time, the bulk of the equity portfolio—say at least 60 percent—should be in North American issues, simply because the risks are lower investing closer to home.

Some gold funds still invest principally in South Africa—and these may be interesting vehicles should the country's shares be rerated upwards reflecting the success of hoped for political and social changes. One such fund is ASA, a closed-end investment company which trades on the New York Stock Exchange. Tables 10.1–10.3 list only open-end mutual funds. Ask your broker to get more information, including the latest annual and quarterly reports, for the funds which may be of interest to you—and read them carefully before investing.

AT least 60% should be in North American issues, — risks are lower investing closer to home.

11
Speculating in
Gold Futures

Introduction

So you want to make a killing in gold. Then the futures market may be for you. Nowhere else are the potential rewards as great for the gold investor. Fortunes will be made here by the most savvy traders and speculators during the next major bull market in gold.

But beware, the risks are equally as great—and fortunes will be lost here, as well. The significant potential for both gains and losses arises from the leverage available to the investor and speculator. Unless you're one of the few successful speculators, chances are you'll lose your shirt.

Keep in mind, that trading gold futures is no substitute for investing in gold coins, bullion, gold mining shares, or mutual funds. Futures traders willingly accept great risks for the opportunity of achieving great rewards. But investing in coins, bullion, gold mining shares, and mutual funds are often part of a conservative, prudent investment program.

Still, for the aggressive investor willing to take some risks and willing to follow some commonsense trading rules, gold futures can be a profitable arena. This chapter is intended to introduce the newcomer to gold futures trading. Once you've learned these basics, if you intend to trade futures, I'd recommend you read up further.

Hedgers and Speculators

Although commodity exchanges—or futures exchanges, which is what we are really talking about—have the image of a gambling casino to many uninformed observers, they were established to serve legitimate commercial needs of the various businesses dealing in gold and the other commodities which are traded on futures exchanges.

For example, farmers, food processors, and merchants use these markets, to hedge their price risk. A farmer in Minnesota may sell wheat futures when he plants his crop to assure a profitable price months later when the harvest is reaped and delivered to his customer, perhaps a flour milling company. Similarly, mining companies may presell their production in order to guarantee a minimum price and rate of profit. Jewelers may buy gold futures to lock in their raw materials costs months before actual fabrication so that they can publish a catalog with set prices, confident that even if the price of gold rises sharply they will make a profit. Similarly, a bullion dealer or refiner with a large inventory of bullion may sell gold futures contracts to hedge against a declining price that would erode the value of its inventory position.

Unlike the hedger, a speculator is an individual or company that has no commercial interest in buying or selling physical gold. Instead, the speculator has an opinion on the direction of gold prices and tries to profit from any changes. If, as a speculator, you believe that gold will rise in price, you might buy gold futures contracts in the hopes of selling later at a higher price. If you believe that the metal's price is heading down, you might sell futures contracts with the intention of buying them back at a lower price.

Hedgers and speculators both play vital roles in gold futures trading—hedgers by producing, processing, merchandising, and consuming physical gold, and speculators by assuming the price risk which commercial hedgers are striving to avoid. This transfer of risk from hedgers to speculators is one of the chief economic benefits of futures markets. In addition, speculators and investors serve an important function by increasing market liquidity and assuring that commercial participants can easily execute their desired trades.

Every gold futures transaction involves two traders—one who is going *long* by entering into a contract to take delivery of gold at some future date and another who is going *short* by promising to deliver gold at some future date. Moreover, in the jargon of a mathematician, the futures market is a zero-sum game, since each contract represents equal and opposite long and short positions. In other words, for every winner, there is a loser; for every dollar made by one trader, a dollar will be lost by another.

The History of Futures Trading
in the United States

In the early 1800s, it was common for farmers to bring their goods to
regional markets at a given time of the year following harvests or when
their livestock was ready for slaughter. But prices were often so unpre-
dictable that farmers and their customers began to make contracts ahead
of time—a practice which began in Chicago soon after the city's founding
in 1833. This was a form of hedging, very much like the system whereby
the modern-day futures exchanges allow participants to buy and sell
commodities in advance of production or use. It was not until the mid-
1800s, around the time of the Civil War, that these forward contracts,
known as *to-arrive* contracts, became codified and standardized on the
Chicago Board of Trade.

The concept of trading futures was later adopted in New York. Initially, metals such as tin, silver, and copper were traded along with other
commodities such as rubber, silk, and hides. Producers and industrial
buyers of these commodities now had an opportunity to hedge their
business commitments and, at the same time, investors and traders had a
new arena for speculation.

Just as the ownership and trading of physical gold by private individuals had been banned in the United States in 1933, there was likewise a
legal proscription against gold futures trading. Even before 1933, however, gold futures were not traded in this country, largely because the
buying and selling of gold was dominated by the London-based bullion
houses. It was not until the start of 1975, when the ban on private gold
ownership was lifted, that gold futures trading began on several competing U.S. futures exchanges. By the end of the decade, the Commodity
Exchange Inc. in New York—COMEX, for short—had emerged as the
leading gold futures exchange.

Although gold futures are traded on a number of other exchanges
around the world—in Tokyo, Hong Kong, Sidney, and Sao Paolo—the
world's largest and most important gold futures exchange is New York's
COMEX. Throughout this book, I'll be describing gold futures as they are
traded on the COMEX.

Gold Futures Defined

First, just what are gold futures contracts? Gold futures contracts traded
on COMEX are legal commitments to make or accept delivery of 100
ounces of gold during a specific month in the future and at an agreed

upon price. The gold must be in the standard form approved by the exchange, i.e., one 100-ounce bar or three kilobars of 0.995 purity or better, fabricated by an exchange-approved refiner. Since all gold futures contracts traded on COMEX are standardized, the only negotiable aspect is the price, which is determined at the time of the trade by the mutual agreement of both buyer and seller, or their representatives, on the floor of the exchange.

Although you've agreed to take or make delivery of 100 ounces of gold for every contract you've bought or sold, its highly unlikely your contract will result in physical delivery of gold bullion. Instead, at some point prior to the contract's maturity, you'll almost certainly offset your initial position with an opposite trade. Less than 3 percent of all futures contracts traded each year actually result in delivery of the underlying commodity. The difference between your original purchase or sale price and the price of the offsetting trade represents the realized profit or loss. (If you choose to take delivery—and for some investors this may be a convenient mechanism for acquiring gold bullion—you'll receive a warehouse or depository receipt attesting to the fact that you own a particular bar or bars in a particular COMEX-approved depository.)

Reading the Futures Price Table

There's a few more things you need to know before I take you through a typical transaction. First, take a look at futures price tables published in your daily newspaper, in *The Wall Street Journal*, or in *Barron's* financial weekly—and find the section for COMEX gold prices. A sample is reproduced in Fig. 11.1. Prices are reported for each contract month traded on COMEX. The contract months are listed in the left-hand column. For each month, the day's opening price, high, low, and settling or closing price are reported; in addition, the change from the prior day's settlement price is shown along with the highest and lowest price recorded so far during the life of the contract, that is, since trading for delivery in the given month first began; finally, the open interest for each contract month is reported.

Open interest is the total number of contracts that have been opened— and have not yet been liquidated either by an offsetting futures contract or by delivery. Each open contract simultaneously represents the long position of one trader and the short position of another trader. Along with the volume of contracts traded—which is reported with one day's lag at the bottom of the table—open interest is an indicator of activity and liquidity.

Figure 11.1. Sample gold futures price table.

	Open	High	Low	Settle	Change	Lifetime High	Low	Open Interest
GOLD (CMX) — 100 troy oz.; $ per troy oz.								
Feb	353.20	354.10	353.30	353.00	− .40	456.50	348.50	295
Apr	354.20	355.30	353.80	354.50	− .20	446.00	350.70	55,396
June	356.20	357.20	356.10	356.60	− .20	467.00	353.80	16,021
Aug	358.60	359.30	358.30	358.70	− .20	426.50	355.00	6,704
Oct	....	....		360.80	− .20	410.80	358.50	2,291
Dec	363.50	363.50	362.50	363.10	− .10	431.00	359.40	4,676
Fb93	....	....		365.40	− .10	404.20	366.70	7,048
Apr	....	....		367.80	− .10	410.00	368.50	5,843
June	....	....		370.30	− .10	418.50	366.00	2,846
Aug	....	....		373.10	− .10	395.50	374.10	1,401
Oct	....	....		376.00	− .10	395.00	378.70	337
Dec	378.60	378.60	378.60	378.90	− .10	402.80	374.50	1,266
Ju95	....	....		388.60	− .10	....	....	100
Dec	....	....		398.80	− .10	....	....	100

Est vol 21,000; vol Tues 28,285; open int 104,268, +3,795.

Notice that the settlement price for each consecutive month is slightly higher than the preceding month. This rising price trend is called the *contango*. In the gold market, the price difference or contango between any two delivery months always equals the cost of financing, storing, and insuring gold for the time interval between the contract month delivery dates. Whenever prices begin to diverge from the appropriate contango, arbitrage by bullion dealers will bring prices back into line.

The Clearinghouse

Overseeing the operation of a commodity futures exchange is the *clearinghouse*. This is an organization associated with the exchange that is responsible for processing all trades and assuring that sufficient margin is deposited by all participants to guarantee the integrity of the exchange and assure fulfillment of all contractual obligations by the exchange members and participants.

The clearinghouse may be a separate corporation in which the exchange's *clearing members* are shareholders, as is the case with COMEX, or it may be a unit of the exchange itself, as is the case with some other commodity markets. The clearinghouse is responsible for keeping track of every trade on the exchange and matching up the participating firms in each transaction.

At the end of each trading day, the clearinghouse notifies its member firms of their net margin requirements based upon all of the long and short positions of each firm's customers. (Each brokerage firm is responsible for keeping track of their own customer's trades and net positions.) The clearinghouse also handles notices of intentions to make delivery on behalf of the holders of short positions from each firm. These delivery notices are given to those member firms which, according to clearinghouse records, have held their long positions for the greatest amount of time. These firms, in turn, pass on these delivery notices to their own customers with the oldest long contracts.

Leverage and Margin

The leverage—and, hence, the potential for great profits or losses—arises from the fact that you control 100 ounces of gold for only a fraction of its current value. When you enter into a contract to buy (or sell) 100 ounces of gold, you're not actually required to pay for the gold until the contract matures. Instead, on the trade date, whether you are a buyer or a seller, you will be required to make a good faith or initial margin payment with your broker. (Your broker will, in turn, be required to deposit margin with the exchange's clearinghouse on the net short or long position among all of its customers' outstanding positions.)

Margin on futures contracts is much different from margin paid on equity transactions. Margin on stock purchases is a down payment by the investor—with the brokerage firm extending the investor credit and charging interest on the unpaid balance. Margin on gold futures transactions is not a down payment since the bullion is not actually purchased or sold unless delivery occurs. Instead, margin on futures contracts are a good faith payment or performance bond intended to guarantee that the investor will honor his contractual obligation. Since your broker is not extending credit, no interest charges will be incurred.

Minimum initial margin requirements are set by COMEX based on the recent historical volatility of gold prices at percentages likely to exceed the daily price movement of a gold futures contract. Margin deposits are adjusted daily to reflect the last day's change in the price of gold. If the gold price moves against your position, your broker will require additional *variation* margin be paid. Similarly, funds will be credited to your account if the gold price moves in your favor. As I'll explain later, these credits can be withdrawn as cash profits or credited to new futures positions, allowing you to pyramid gains into spectacular profits.

A Typical Transaction

If you're bullish and expect an imminent rise in the price of gold you can buy a gold futures contract. By acquiring a long futures position, you will have become a speculator betting on an upward move in the metal's price. But if you're wrong and the market moves against you, your initial investment can quickly be lost. Experienced traders know how to protect themselves using stops and other strategies which are discussed later in the chapter.

Here are the steps in a hypothetical trade: You call your broker and instruct him to purchase, on your behalf, several contracts on COMEX for delivery six months hence. In this example, assume the spot price of gold is $350 an ounce and the price for delivery in six months is $367 an ounce, the premium for future delivery being the contango which we have discussed. You have decided to buy 10 contracts—altogether representing 1000 ounces—with a total value of $367,000 ($367 × 100 ounces per contract × 10 contracts). Seems like a big investment—but thanks to the low initial margin requirements you will need to make an outlay of only 5 to 10 percent. In this case, your broker asks for 5 percent—only $18,350, as initial margin.

Day by day, the price of gold moves higher. You're feeling pretty good about your decision to speculate in gold futures. After a month, the metal has moved up to $380 an ounce and the price of your futures contract is now $395. In total, your ten contracts are trading at $395,000—an increase of $28,000.

At any point, when the market is moving with your position, you have three choices:

1. If you're happy with the gain and believe that gold's prospects are changing, you can take your profits. Call your broker, liquidate your position, and receive a check in the mail or a credit to your brokerage account of $28,000. Thanks to the leverage of futures markets, this is a gain of 52 percent on your initial investment of $18,350.

2. If you think that gold is going higher, you can leave your position alone and let your profits accumulate—that is if you're right and the metal continues to appreciate. In this case, if you want, you can ask your broker to pay you the excess of the current minimum margin on your 10 contracts and the increase in the market value of the position. Five percent minimum margin (0.05 × $395,000) is $19,750—so you can withdraw $8250 ($28,000 − $19,750).

3. Use this gain as initial margin on an additional futures position. This

strategy makes sense for the aggressive speculator who is confident that gold is still going higher. You call your broker with instructions to buy four more futures contracts at $395. Your past gain is enough to cover the initial margin requirement for the new contracts (0.05 × $395 × four contracts × 100 ounces per contract) of $7900. Now your long position totals 14 contracts and you stand to make even more if gold keeps rising. As long as the market continues to move in the right direction, you can continue reinvesting your profits into additional futures positions. This practice of increasing you position with existing gains is called *pyramiding*.

In this hypothetical situation, everything worked to your advantage. But suppose you were wrong—at least in the short term. Instead of moving higher, gold reacted poorly to some bearish news and its price fell sharply just after you went long. Your broker will soon be on the phone asking you for additional variation margin. And, if you're unwilling or unable to make this additional good faith deposit, the brokerage firm will have no choice but to liquidate your position.

Remember, you bought 10 gold futures contracts at $367 an ounce: The total value of your position was $367,000 but your initial margin payment was only $18,350, or 5 percent of the total value of the position. By the next day, gold has closed down $8 an ounce. Your 10-contract position has depreciated by $8000 ($8 × 10 contracts × 100 ounces per contract)—and your broker is asking for an $8000 check.

If you fail to pay, your position will be sold for $359,000 assuming gold is still down by $8 an ounce, and you'll receive a check from your broker for $10,350 (your initial margin minus $8000) less any additional commissions that are due. In a day, you've seen your investment fall by 44 percent.

Tools of the Trade

The day-to-day volatility of gold prices, in combination with the leverage of futures markets, makes this a high-risk arena for only the most intrepid speculators. Even if your view of the market is correct in the medium to longer term, your initial investment, plus any variation margin that you may have deposited with your broker, can be lost within days.

The bullish premise of this book is built on fundamental analysis of prospective trends in gold's supply and demand. But most successful futures traders rely on technical analysis for short-term trading signals. If you are contemplating trading gold futures, I'd advise that you first learn the basics of technical analysis to help determine the timing of your trades. Technicians rely on analysis of past price movements for clues about prospective price movements. See Chap. 15 for "An Introduction to Technical Analysis."

To win the gold futures trading game takes three things:

1. A correct view of the underlying price trend

2. A sense of timing and short-term price prospects—that is knowing when to implement positions and when to liquidate them

3. The discipline to quickly cut ones losses in order to preserve your investment capital when the market moves against you

In fact, some successful traders have no opinion beyond the next few minutes, hours, or days—profiting only from their uncanny sense about the market's near-term direction, something which may have little or nothing to do with fundamentals and economics.

As a rule, you should be willing and able to absorb a number of small trading loses in order to have the opportunity to score big gains when the market moves in your favor. In other words, limit your losses. The best way to do this is to have predetermined points at which your position will be liquidated if the price of gold moves against you. In the jargon of futures markets, these points are called *stops*. A stop, or stop-loss order, is a resting order left with your broker to liquidate a long position if the price drops to a certain level or, in the case of a short position, if the price rises to a certain level.

There are a number of ways to implement or liquidate futures positions:

A *market order* is one which will be executed on your behalf by your broker's floor trader at the prevailing market price when the order reaches the exchange floor.

A *stop order* is one which will not be executed until the market reaches a specified price. A stop order can be used to buy or sell, to initiate a new position, or liquidate an old one. A stop order to buy is initiated above the current market price. A stop order to sell is initiated below the current market price. Once the designated price point in a stop order is reached, the floor broker will execute it as soon as possible.

A *limit order* also instructs the floor broker at what specific price point to enter the market. Unlike stop orders, however, which may be executed at any price above or below the stop point once the point is touched, a limit order may be exercised at the limit or better. For example, a limit order to buy may be executed at or below the specified price; a limit order to sell may be executed at or above the specified price.

Stop-limit orders become activated when the market reaches the specified stop price, but the floor trader is limited to a maximum price if you are buying and a minimum price if you are selling.

A *market-if-touched order* is an order that must be filled once the specified price is touched, but unlike a limit order, it must be executed even if the market subsequently reverses.

Generally speaking, unless otherwise specified, orders remain good for one day, at the end of which all unfilled orders expire. You can, however, designate an order as "good for the week." Or you can ask your broker to reenter the order week after week until it is executed.

An alternative is the *fill or kill order*—which will be executed immediately by the floor broker at the specified price or better, or will not be exercised at all. You can specify orders that must be executed on the open or close of the day. A *market on open order* must be executed, if possible, during the officially designated opening period. Similarly, a *market on close order* must be executed, if possible, during the officially designated closing period.

These various mechanisms for initiating orders or liquidating positions give the speculator, who is not on the floor of the exchange, the opportunity to specify under exactly what circumstances he would like the trade executed. They are used most effectively in tandem with technical analysis which can help the astute trader and chartist pick the moments at which to enter and exit the market.

Day Trading vs. Position Taking

Commodity futures markets, especially the gold futures market, can be active and fast moving. A profit or loss amounting to thousands of dollars is possible within a very short time. For the trader with access to *real time* market information—that is, a computer screen or wire service such as Reuters—day trading in gold futures is possible and can be highly rewarding. But unless you are willing to devote a significant amount of time, energy, and money to day trading, it is something best left to professionals.

Because the speculator's exposure in day trading is limited, the margin requirements normally are lower than for *position* trades which are held overnight or for longer periods. In fact, many brokerage firms charge day traders lower commissions because they usually trade more often than speculators taking longer-term positions.

Floor brokers trading for their own accounts are often satisfied with profits of a dollar or less on a particular trade, entering and exiting the market sometimes frequently over the course of the day, perhaps trading the long side of the market in the morning and then shorting gold in the afternoon. Such frequent day trading, whether conducted by a floor broker or by an outside speculator is known as *scalping* the market.

Most of us, however, have other professions and interests—making successful day trading and scalping impossible. We must be content to position trade, taking positions that we will hold for days, weeks, or even months.

Taking Delivery

The gold futures market offers investors and speculators an arena for risk taking and, potentially, for achieving great profits. COMEX also offers an excellent mechanism for acquiring physical gold for those who can afford 100 ounces, the minimum quantity represented by one futures contract.

After a fashion, buying gold on COMEX and taking delivery is akin to buying wholesale—since the COMEX price does not reflect any service fees, bar fabrication costs, or other charges you may be subject to if you buy through a retail bullion dealer. Commissions paid for entering into a futures contract are far more reasonable, perhaps only $20 a contract at a discount broker or $100 a contract at a full service broker, compared with several hundred dollars in commissions and charges on the purchase of a 100-ounce bar.

By entering into a long gold futures contract and standing for delivery upon the contract's expiration, you will receive a warehouse receipt representing your ownership of gold bullion held at one of the COMEX-approved bullion depositories. Then you can choose to leave it in the warehouse, making arrangements to pay standard storage fees, have the bullion shipped to another bullion storage facility, or take delivery of the metal yourself.

Summary

Markets are dynamic—and if you are trading gold futures, your strategy needs to be flexible, as well as responsive, to the changing market circumstances. If you are long, ask yourself daily whether this is still an appropriate position based on long-term fundamentals as well as the short-term technical picture. If the price is moving in your favor, periodically raise your stops—the points at which you will liquidate positions to limit losses (or take profits) should the market reverse.

The leveraged nature of gold futures markets and the ability to pyramid profits into ever-larger positions could make a few smart traders very wealthy during the next big bull market in gold. But the risks are equally as great and many players will lose big money through inappropriate or unwise trading—or just by being unlucky. However, there are other ways to profit from a bull market without exposure to the risks of futures markets. Equities and gold oriented mutual funds have already been discussed. For those who want bigger potential gains without the big risks of gold futures, options—on equities, bullion, and futures—may be the answer.

12
Using Options on Futures and Equities

Introduction

So far, we have reviewed gold coins, bullion, mining shares, mutual funds, and futures. Options contracts to buy or sell bullion, mining shares, or futures are yet another vehicle for the gold investor and speculator. Options combine the opportunity for big profits but the risks, unlike the risks to futures traders, are predefined and limited to your initial investment.

Years ago, options had their roots in the real estate arena, where in return for a cash payment a developer received the right from a property owner to buy land at a specified price anytime within a specified time period. If the developer decided, for whatever reason, not to acquire the property—perhaps he could not get financing or the zoning variances needed for a proposed project—he lost only the initial cash cost of the option. The owner benefited as well—although the property remained unsold, he did manage to derive some income from his ownership position.

Like the real estate option, options on gold, mining equities, and other investment assets give potential buyers the opportunity to lock in a price on a prospective investment purchase for a period of time. And, they also give the holders of these assets the opportunity to generate additional income. Options on gold and a wide range of investment assets and financial vehicles have evolved into sophisticated media serving a variety of purposes, from hedging to speculation. As with futures, this chapter is meant to be a basic primer. Before you dive into the option market it would be wise to do some additional reading.

Options Defined

An *options contract* is an agreement giving the buyer of the option the right—but not the obligation—to buy or sell an underlying asset, within some specified time frame, at a specified price from the seller of the option. If the buyer (or *holder*) of the option decides to exercise his right to buy or sell the underlying asset, the seller (also known as the *writer* or *grantor*) of the option is obligated to turn over or accept the asset at the previously agreed-upon price. An option that is not exercised within a specified time frame simply expires worthless.

Today, options are traded on a wide array of investment assets and financial instruments—but our area of interest is options on bullion, gold mining shares, and futures contracts.

The price of an option—the amount of money paid by the buyer to the seller of the option—is called the *premium*. The predetermined price at which an option to buy or sell the underlying asset can be exercised prior to its expiration date is called the *strike price*.

Options come in two varieties: *calls* and *puts*. The holder of a call has the right to buy the underlying asset at the stated strike price on or before the expiry date. A put option gives the holder the right to sell the underlying asset at the stated strike price on or before the expiry date. In either case, the writer or grantor of the option must fulfill his contractual obligation to sell (in the case of a call) or buy (in the case of a put).

Options are identified by the name of their underlying asset, the maturity month of the option, and its strike price. For example, an option to buy a February COMEX gold futures contract at $400 an ounce would be known as a COMEX February 400 call; an option to sell 100 shares of Echo Bay Mines at $7 a share between now and next June would be known as an Echo Bay June 7 put.

Understanding Options Pricing

The price or cost of an option is known as the premium. For exchange-traded options, this price is determined by a competitive auction on the floor of a stock or commodity exchange. (Dealer options which are written, traded, and marketed by gold dealers are not discussed here, although the general principles are much the same.)

In theory, options premiums have two components—its *intrinsic value* and the *time value* of the option. The intrinsic value is the amount by which the underlying asset price (for the stock or futures contract, for example) is above a call option's strike price or below a put option's strike price. This is equivalent to the option's market value at exercise. Any option which has intrinsic value is said to be *in-the-money*. An option without intrinsic value is *out-of-the-money*. If the current price of the underlying asset is the same as the strike price, the option is *at-the-money* and has no intrinsic value.

Often, an option will trade at more than its intrinsic value. This difference, known as the *option's time value*, is the additional amount that buyers are willing to pay in the expectation that the option's intrinsic value will increase prior to expiration. This, in turn, is related to:

- The time left before maturity—the more time, the more value—because of the increased probability that the intrinsic value will increase before expiration. As the expiration date of an option approaches, the time value diminishes.

- The price volatility of the underlying asset—the higher the volatility, the more value. If the underlying asset has recently experienced relatively large swings up and down in its price, in other words, has exhibited a high degree of price volatility, the greater probability will be that the intrinsic value will increase during the time remaining before expiration.

- The interest and other costs of carrying the underlying asset—since this is a cost to the arbitrageurs who will try to profit from any discrepancies in the theoretical relationship between the prices of the underlying asset and the option itself.

- And, in the case of equity options, the expectations of any dividend that may be paid.

Professional options traders use sophisticated computer models to calculate the theoretical price of an option based on these variables. When the actual market price diverges from their calculated theoretical price, professional traders will attempt to profit from the expectation that this divergence will be short lived. As a result, the premiums for all actively traded options will be close to their theoretical values. As an investor, your interest is not to trade based on small discrepancies in premiums—but to use options to achieve leverage with limited risk or possibly to generate additional income from your portfolio.

The Choices

In the United States, options are available on bullion, a variety of gold mining stocks, an index representing a basket of gold and silver mining stocks, and gold futures contracts. If you're an investor contemplating trading options, I recommend you stick to exchange-traded options on individual equities and/or COMEX gold futures contracts. These are the most liquid and meet the needs of most investors, speculators, and traders.

Options on a number of major North American gold mining equities are traded on various U.S. exchanges. Glance through the equity market options price tables listed in *The Wall Street Journal* daily or *Barron's* weekly and you can see which equity options are available on each exchange. Options are available on such well known mining equities including ASA, American Barrick, Battle Mountain, Echo Bay, Homestake Mining, Newmont Gold, Newmont Mining, Pegasus, and Placer Dome. You can also buy and sell options representing an index of gold and silver mining stocks. This index option is traded on the Philadelphia Stock Exchange.

In the United States, bullion options are available from one major dealer but are marketed through a number of other commodity and brokerage firms. These options are not exchange traded and they are not recommended because they are dependent on the creditworthiness of the issuing dealer, and because the prices are not readily available in the daily newspapers. In addition to these dealer options, bullion options are traded on exchanges in Amsterdam, Montreal, and Vancouver. COMEX gold options (discussed below), offer American investors a good alternative to both dealer options and these foreign exchange traded options.

Finally, options on COMEX gold futures contracts have been traded on that exchange since 1982, and offer gold investors and speculators interested in options the best overall vehicle. Remember, the holder of a gold futures contract has, in theory, virtually unlimited risk. In reality, the use of stops as discussed in Chap. 11 can minimize these risks. Nevertheless, without protective strategies, the market can go against your futures position, whether it be short or long, for an indefinite period and subject you to margin calls. By contrast, the options buyer pays only the initial premium and never faces any margin calls. The risk is limited to the loss of the premium if the option expires out-of-the-money.

In 1991, COMEX launched trading in a 5-day gold option. Each 5-day put and call option expires just five days after it is listed and begins trading on the exchange. Strike prices are set so that the options begin trading *at-the-money*. These are intended to offer short-term traders an economical instrument for speculation. Their short maturities means that these options have little time value. At expiration, the options are settled in cash—so that there is no underlying asset to deliver.

Reading the Options Price Table

Before I take you through the mechanics of some simple options trading strategies, there is one more thing you need to know: how to read the options price tables published in your daily paper, *The Wall Street Journal*, and in *Barron's* financial weekly. A sample reporting COMEX gold options is reproduced in Fig. 12.1. Notice, first of all, that the table lists puts and calls separately. Premiums (or prices) for each strike price and expiration date are reported. Daily (or weekly) volume and open interest are also given for all calls and all puts traded. Equity options tables are sometimes presented in the newspapers differently. You will have to scan through the options tables for each exchange printed in your newspaper to find the listings for each mining company. Several options with different strike prices may be listed.

As with futures contracts, open interest is the total number of options

Figure 12.1. Sample gold options price table.

```
             -METALS-

GOLD (CMX)
  100 troy ounces; $ per troy ounce
Strike   Calls-Settle       Puts-Settle
Price  Apr  May   Jun  Apr  May   Jun
330   24.70 27.20 27.20  .20   .60  1.10
340   15.20 17.90 18.60  .70  1.30  2.20
350    6.80  9.90 11.20 2.30  3.30  4.70
360    1.70  4.30  5.60 7.20  7.70  9.10
370     .60  1.80  2.80 16.10 15.20 16.00
380     .30   .80  1.40 25.70 24.20 24.50
   Est. vol. 3,500;
Tues vol. 2,026 calls; 2,780 puts
Op. Int. Tues 78,696 calls; 23,517 puts
SILVER (CMX)
  5,000 troy ounces; cts per troy
ounce
```

contracts that are outstanding. Along with sales or volume of contracts traded, which is also reported with one day's lag, open interest is a measure of market activity and liquidity.

There is a wide range of options trading, speculating, and hedging strategies. Generally speaking, you will be interested in:

- Buying calls if you think prices are going higher.

- Selling covered calls if you own the underlying asset and wish to enhance your returns at times when you believe prices will be stagnant or declining.

- Possibly buying puts to hedge against a fall in the price of your bullion, mining shares, or futures position.

Some traders will also sell or write *naked* options. These are uncovered in the sense that the trader does not own the underlying asset—and theoretically has unlimited risk should he be required to make delivery. Naked options strategies are not appropriate for most investors and speculators, and, therefore, are not discussed any further in this book.

I'll begin with two of the more popular strategies for the individual investor. Although COMEX options are used to illustrate the first example and equity options the second, these strategies apply equally to all types of gold-related options vehicles.

Buying Call Options— A Typical Transaction

In the simplest case, if you anticipate an imminent rise in the price of gold, call options are a good vehicle for achieving leverage with limited downside risk. The buyer of a COMEX gold option, for example, can control a futures contract with only a small premium outlay. And, the risk is limited to the initial cost of the option, that is, the premium plus any brokerage commissions.

For example, you've called your broker and instructed him to buy 10 December 380s. December gold is trading on COMEX at $365 an ounce. These options are out-of-the-money, since the strike price is above the current market price of the underlying asset. These options won't begin to earn money for you until the market price of the December gold futures contract exceeds the options strike price by at least the amount paid for the option—your initial premium plus commissions. Being out-of-the-money, the options have no intrinsic value and the cost was only

$0.90 an ounce. In total, your 10 options cost $900 (10 options × 100 ounces per contract × $0.90 an ounce) plus commissions, not a big sum to pay for the potential gain on 1000 ounces of gold.

You've got until December, when the option expires, to exercise. That's still some months away. Luckily, you were right in your forecast of higher gold prices. Week by week the price climbs. By late November, the price of a December contract has risen to $399 an ounce—a gain of $34, or roughly 9 percent. Meanwhile, your option has moved into the money, now that the market price of December gold is above the strike price. The option price has advanced from $0.90 an ounce to $19.50—that's a gain of $18.60 an ounce. Excluding commissions, you've earned $18,600 on your 10 options contracts. As you can see, buying out-of-the-money calls with low premiums offers the potential of really fantastic gains if the market makes a big move in your favor. Had gold failed to move above $380 (the strike price), the option would have expired worthless and you would have lost your $900 initial outlay.

Hedging with Options

You may already own gold bullion, futures, or equities—or you may be just initiating a new long position in one of these vehicles. You're bullish but worried about a possible near-term decline. Buying puts in conjunction with ownership of the underlying asset may give you just the insurance policy you'd like against price erosion, without sacrificing any of the upside potential should the market really take off.

In this example, you just bought 1000 shares of Homestake Mining. At $15 a share, your total outlay was $15,000. Homestake is considered by some analysts as one of the gold stocks likely to appreciate most rapidly when gold begins to move higher; as a relatively high-cost, unhedged producer, their earnings should benefit greatly from a higher gold price. But you're worried about the timing. Perhaps a newsletter writer (whose views you respect) or your broker thinks gold may move down one more time. So you buy Homestake puts to protect against a falling price. Homestake January 15 puts cost $1 a share—or $1000 to protect your whole investment from now until next January 15th.

If gold moves higher, Homestake will appreciate and your investment will perform well. However, by mid-January, the put option will be worthless. On the other hand, say your broker was right. Gold has fallen sharply and Homestake unfortunately is down to $9 a share. Not to worry, however. Although your Homestake is off by $6 a share, the premium on the put has moved from $1 to $6.50 a share and this gain nearly offsets the loss on the underlying stock.

These are strategies for the bullish investor. Buying calls or buying puts along with a long position in the underlying asset gives you plenty of upside potential if you are right about the market. But in either case your loss is limited to the option premium paid at the outset.

Income Generation Using Options

A third use of options—generating income—involves the writing or granting of covered options, that is, when you own the underlying asset. This technique allows you to generate returns from an investment asset— such as gold bullion—which pays no interest. Incidentally, a number of central banks of different countries around the world regularly write calls on some portion of their official gold reserves in order to generate a return on their bullion holdings. Covered call options may also be written to enhance the return on dividend-yielding gold mining stocks you may own.

Writers of call options receive income in the form of the premium paid by the buyer. In return, they are giving up the potential appreciation above the option's strike price. Say, for example, that you own 100 shares in Placer Dome. The stock is trading at $16 a share—and you sell a covered call with a strike price of $20 and an expiration date three months hence. The premium on the call is, in this hypothetical example, $1.50— so your income from selling the call is $150 ($1.50 × 100 shares). You retain the opportunity to gain $4 a share (the difference between the current share price and the option's strike price) over the next three months. But if the stock price rises over $20 a share, the stock will be called away from you and any appreciation over this level will be lost. If the stock price remains under the strike price during the life of the option, you will retain ownership of your 100 shares in Placer Dome and you will again benefit from any future appreciation.

If you are writing call options on mining equities or gold futures contracts, remember that you should own the underlying stock or futures position—that is, write covered calls. Your broker will require the deposit of the underlying asset with his firm to guarantee your options contract. If you are writing naked options, which is an ill-advised strategy for most investors, a margin payment will be required.

It is sometimes advisable to write covered calls that are way out-of-the-money since these may appear to be the least likely to be exercised—but they will also have the least intrinsic value. You might want to look for the options which have the longest maturities in order to benefit from their greater time value. However, depending on your view of market prospects, you might feel comfortable writing covered options with strike prices not too far above the current price of the underlying asset (particularly if you believe that the gold price or stock price is due for a short-term correction) and/or with a nearer expiration date.

If the market moves against your options position, you can always offset the position by buying the option back at a loss. This loss, however, will be offset—at least on paper—by the gain in the price of the futures contract or mining stock.

Summary

If you are a serious investor or trader—whether in bullion, mining equities, or futures contracts—you should take a close look at options markets and strategies as a method of increasing returns. There are many varieties of options strategies that are appropriate for aggressive speculators, traders, and more conservative investors. Some offer opportunities for big gains, others provide protection against loss or allow the holder of the underlying asset to generate additional current income, and some strategies may be employed by gold bears anticipating a market decline.

PART 3
Guidelines for Smart Investors

13
The Gold-Plated Portfolio

Introduction

After more than a decade and a half of legalized ownership in the United States, gold still remains a mysterious and misunderstood medium to most American investors. While many investors still scorn gold, gold shares, and other related assets as unconventional, nontraditional—and hence unfit—there is no single asset, looked at globally and historically, that can be more appropriately considered *traditional*.

In my view, gold is the most traditional of all investments. After all, gold's investment tradition spans millennia. The choice of emperors, kings, sultans and sheiks, gold also has been the preferred investment of millions of less well-heeled individuals since time immemorial.

Today, the central banks of nearly every country from Argentina to Zimbabwe, and from the USA to the newly independent republics of Eastern Europe, hold gold bullion as official reserve assets. Likewise, many of the world's wealthiest individuals and families—from the descendents of the robber barons to the takeover kings of Wall Street—own some gold bullion as a prudent investment for all time.

Portfolio Enhancement Using Gold

Some investors hold gold believing it sacrosanct, the one secure asset in an insecure world. Fearful that conventional financial assets, even our very currency, are in dire jeopardy and that hyperinflation or worse lies ahead, gold bugs put their trust in gold. But the individual investor and professional money manager need not rely on the logic or emotion of the gold bug—for gold investment is supported by a cool, objective analysis of the metal's investment attributes, from the lessons of modern portfolio theory, and from experience.

Portfolio theory counsels the investor not only to pursue maximum return, but also to seek minimum variance—that is, reduced exposure to one-sided risk. A central tenet of modern portfolio theory, the *efficient portfolio* concept, focuses on the belief that risk can be minimized through diversification. A portfolio can be made *efficient* by minimizing the risk associated with a given level of return.

An efficient portfolio is achieved through diversification. Moreover, the risk associated with a portfolio can be brought down to a very low level, theoretically approaching zero, if that portfolio consists of two groups of assets whose behavior is negatively correlated. That is, an astute portfolio manager can minimize the chance that the overall portfolio value will be adversely affected by economic and political events by including an asset which performs differently from the conventional stocks, bonds, and other financial assets that would typically comprise his investment holdings.

This brings me to the unique role that gold and gold-related assets can play in achieving an optimally diversified portfolio. Gold possesses a rare and desired quality—in the jargon of investment theorists, a *negative beta*. In plain English, this simply means that the metal's price frequently moves contrary to (or at least independent of) the prices of conventional financial assets. It is precisely this difference in the behavior of the yellow metal versus nongold equities and fixed income instruments that provides the greatest incentive for individual investors and professional money managers to include gold and gold shares in a diversified portfolio.

It is gold's *contrariness* as an investment that commends it as a valuable instrument for *portfolio hedging*. Portfolio hedging is defined as an investment in any two assets whose price movements are inversely correlated, so that the risks of investment in one are substantially offset by the other. Accordingly, adding gold to a conventional portfolio of stocks and bonds can reduce the overall volatility and risk associated with that portfolio.

To put it another way, gold can act as an insurance policy in case the assumptions used in structuring a portfolio turn out to be incorrect. In a sense, modern portfolio theory provides a more sophisticated rationale for the narrower, but still entirely valid, commonsense perception that owning a certain amount of gold provides important protection against harsh conditions adverse to conventional financial assets.

Although a decision to invest in gold or gold-related assets may be made on the basis of modern portfolio theory, actual investment decisions are often guided by much simpler considerations of a more pragmatic nature. Does a particular asset seem likely to provide a high return at acceptable risk? Are there risks in the economic or political spheres that warrant the inclusion of hedge assets in an investment portfolio? As an investor or portfolio manager, your view of the world at any particular time should govern the proportion of your investment portfolio held in gold bullion.

The Investment Pyramid

Investment counselors often talk of the investment pyramid with the most conservative and safest assets at the base, more speculative holdings in the middle, and the riskiest, least conventional assets at the top. For the average investor the pyramid might typically have diversified mutual funds, U.S. Treasury bills and bonds, and money market funds at the bottom. This would comprise the largest percentage of his investable wealth.

The middle of the pyramid might include individual stocks and bonds, for example. For the average middle-income investor, the pyramid might go no higher. But, for the wealthier investor, farther up we might find various limited partnerships, real estate holdings, options, and other nonconventional investments. Commodity futures and other highly speculative vehicles would be found at the very top.

In keeping with the shape of the pyramid, the largest percentage of the portfolio would be invested in assets at the base with progressively smaller percentages being allocated for the assets in the middle and upper tiers.

Where does gold fit in? I'd put gold bullion and gold coins right down in the base of the pyramid. Gold—in small quantities—is one of the most prudent assets, for the reasons outlined earlier in this chapter. It provides a solid foundation, anchoring the pyramid solidly when ill winds may blow across other investment and financial markets. High-quality gold mining stocks and gold-oriented mutual funds fall into the middle range of the pyramid, while gold futures and options are near the top.

How Much Is Right for You?

There are no golden rules about how much gold to own and include in your investment portfolio. In part, the answer is based on your own comfort level with gold and your own anxieties about the risks to conven-

High-quality gold mining stocks + gold-oriented mutual funds fall into the middle range of the pyramid.

tional assets. In part, the answer depends on the nature of your other holdings and how exposed they might be to the risks against which gold provides insurance. And, in part, the answer will be a function of your overall wealth. The more you've got, the more you ought to put into gold bullion or coins.

Use common sense. Five percent of your investment assets is a good starting point for most people. If you can afford more and feel comfortable with gold, by all means buy more. But much more than 10 percent seems excessive to me. If you're bullish on gold, there may be better ways to benefit from a gold price advance than just owning gold bullion or gold coins—and that, in part, is what this book is about.

much more than 10% seems expensive.

14

Tailoring
Your Own
Gold Investment
Program

This book is about gold investing. I advocate gold for two reasons: First, gold is unparalleled as a portfolio diversifier and insurance policy against certain risks. Second, I expect a bull market in gold and gold-related assets before the end of the decade. Some investors will make big profits by participating in this bull market. You could be one of them.

I believe that gold is indeed for everyone—and that there is a place in your own savings and investment program for gold and gold-related assets. But, just as there is no universal portfolio of stocks and bonds that will be satisfactory for everyone, there is no such thing as a universal gold investment program or portfolio that will meet the needs of all investors.

How much to invest, and in what form, will differ from one investor to the next—depending on wealth, income, investment objectives, desire to avoid or accept risk, willingness and time to manage one's own investment affairs, and, importantly, the investor's personal outlook for the economy, investment markets, and perhaps even world affairs.

If you have not invested in gold before, reading this book is your first step toward implementing a personal gold investment program. But just reading this book is not enough—unless you are already a seasoned gold investor familiar with all of the investment vehicles introduced in this book. The biggest gains will be scored by investors in gold mining equities, gold futures, and options. These can be difficult and risky markets for the uninformed and inexperienced investor. So if you wish to take an aggressive approach, you must be prepared to do your homework. Read special-

The biggest gains will be scored by investors in gold mining equities...

ized books, read company reports, subscribe to investment advisory services that specialize in the various markets of interest to you, and become an educated investor or speculator.

Three Types of Gold Investors

Basically, there are three types of gold investors:

1. *Long-term hoarders* hold gold or related assets for years, perhaps with no intention of ever selling. These investors hold gold as an insurance policy, as a means of diversifying against various financial risks, and as a nest egg or component of their most risk-averse savings. Gold bugs who have an apocalyptic view of the future—expecting high inflation, currency depreciation, financial market turbulence, or worse—hold gold as the one secure asset in an insecure world. But many more cool-headed savers and investors, even those with a positive outlook, also hold gold simply because they can't know for sure what the future holds for their other investment holdings, and they recognize the benefits of a gold-plated portfolio. Almost certainly, the long-term hoarder will choose physical gold—probably bullion coins—as the preferred vehicle.

2. *Medium-term investors* may hold gold for a few months or a few years because they wish to profit from their bullish expectations about the metal's future price. These investors are willing to accept some risk in order to achieve an attractive rate of return in the form of capital gains. For the medium-term investor who buys, holds, and eventually sells at hopefully a big profit, mining shares or mutual funds may be the best vehicle.

3. *Short-term investors* or *speculators* have a view of the future with a time horizon of a few minutes, weeks, or months. These short-term investors are not interested in gold as a safety net or hedge, but as a trading vehicle for short-term gains. Because of the greater leverage, gold futures and options are often preferred.

As an investor, unlike many other aspects of your life, it is appropriate to have a multiple personality. I advocate that every investor and saver allocate some funds to building a long-term, possibly permanent, golden nest egg. Those who share my bullish outlook for gold should also invest in shares or mutual funds. And, the more intrepid may also wish to speculate in futures and options.

Building Your Golden Nest Egg

Physical gold—in coin or bar form—is one of the least risky investments available. And, as I point out in Chap. 13, "The Gold-Plated Portfolio," inclusion of gold in a diversified investment program will reduce the risk and volatility of the entire portfolio.

But what is the best way to buy gold. For the new investor, bullion coins are the single best vehicle. They are easy to buy, easy to resell, easy to transport, and easy to store—and, if you stick with one of the major brands and buy through a reputable dealer, you are not likely to go wrong. In Chap. 8, "Bullion Coins," I advocate that you diversify among the popular national brands to further reduce your risks.

One-ounce coins are also a convenient denomination for building your golden nest egg. You might decide to buy a few—perhaps 10 ounces, 5 ounces, or even just 1 ounce—every month or quarter until you reach your targeted core holding.

Bullion storage programs with nationally recognized brokerage houses or banks are an alternative to coin purchases, particularly if you don't want physical delivery. Many of these financial service firms also offer accumulation programs which are an easy way to build up your core position in gold or to augment it as your income and/or wealth grow over time.

Coins can also be left in a storage account, giving you the option to easily take delivery in the future should you so desire. In either case, make sure the gold is held in a segregated account, not commingled with the broker's or bank's own holdings. This will protect you against any possible default or bankruptcy on the part of the financial service firm you're dealing with.

How Much Is Appropriate?

How much physical gold should you own? The answer varies depending on your own circumstances, investment priorities, and your own view of the world. Many advocates of gold suggest that a small percentage of your investment assets—from 2 to 10 percent—should be in gold bullion or coins.

Within this range, what do you feel comfortable with? How vulnerable are your other assets to the risks against which gold might offer some protection? Do you own a home or other real estate? Is your equity portfolio heavily weighted with natural resource stocks that may do well in an inflationary environment, or utilities that will suffer with a rise in inflation? Although not a substitute for physical gold, do you own any gold mining shares or mutual funds? Do you have a large portfolio of long-term bonds? Have you diversified your investments globally?

There is also a cost to holding gold. It earns no interest—although in a rising market, its price appreciation is a return on your investment. This opportunity cost, in my mind, is equivalent to the premium you'd pay on a casualty or life insurance policy. Generally, the wealthier you are the more insurance you can afford to hold—and this is true of gold as well as other forms of insurance. In other words, the greater your income or wealth, the more you can afford to hold in physical gold, both in absolute terms and as a proportion of your overall investment assets.

As I suggested in Chap. 13, placing 5 percent of your overall investment and savings assets in gold bullion or bullion coins is a good starting point for many investors.

Profiting from a Bull Market

A small position—from 2 to 10 percent of your investment assets—in physical gold is a prudent investment for all time. But there are times— and the mid-1990s may be one such period—when you might wish to bet on a rising gold price. Physical gold—coins and bars—are not the best vehicles for maximizing your returns from a rising gold price.

For the most conservative, risk-averse investor gold-oriented mutual funds make sense. The better-run funds are also attractive to those investors who have neither the time nor the inclination to be actively involved in managing their investments. However, as I discussed in Chap. 10, "Mutual Funds," not all funds are created equal—and it's important to choose a fund that is managed by an experienced team of professionals. If you're a fairly wealthy investor making a substantial commitment to this sector, you might consider diversifying by owning two gold-oriented funds managed by different fund groups.

If you are willing to spend some time doing research and keeping well informed on individual companies, investing directly in mining shares may make sense. Moreover, its possible to enhance your returns by selecting those companies whose profitability and share prices will be most responsive to changes in the gold price. But for many individual investors, actively managing your own gold share portfolio also entails additional risks.

How much should you invest in gold funds or directly in gold mining stocks? Again, the answer will vary from one individual to another. As a general rule, ask yourself what proportion of your portfolio would you be willing to invest in any one industry group or investment sector when you're bullish on that area? Whatever your answer, that's how much you should feel comfortable investing in gold funds or equities.

For the most aggressive investors and speculators, gold futures and options on various gold-related assets offer the potential for tremendous profits—but they also face the equally large risk of losing their entire investment. Nevertheless, it is in these arenas—futures and options— where the biggest fortunes will be made during the next big bull market. How much money should you be willing to devote to trading futures and options? Only as much as you're willing to lose without dire personal financial consequences.

A Commonsense Approach

As I said at the beginning of this chapter, there is no such thing as a universal gold investment program. However, there are some common sense principals that can guide most investors:

1. Buy some physical gold—either bullion or coins—before you do anything else.

2. Choose a good gold-oriented mutual fund. It's better to be early than late and miss the party altogether—so make a small investment in the fund of your choice now.

3. If you are not interested in actively managing your own investments, forget about gold mining stocks, futures, and options. Instead, when you think gold is going to start moving higher, increase your investment in your favorite gold-oriented mutual fund. And, when you're confident gold is in a sustainable bull market, buy still more.

4. If you are somewhat more proactive and enjoy managing your own investment affairs, choose three or four blue chip gold stocks—but only after you've bought physical gold and made an initial gold fund investment. Your gold fund investment should be equal to at least the investment you'd make in any one gold stock, assuming you are choosing three or four companies for your portfolio. Owning a gold fund will also help you track your own performance. Over time, if you are not doing as well as your fund, reduce your equity holdings and increase your gold fund holdings. Wealthier investors with bigger portfolios may want to hold more than three or four individual companies in order to further diversify against the risks associated with any one company.

5. Figure out how much money you are willing to lose in any one-, two-, or three-month period. This is the maximum amount of new funds you should be willing to speculate in gold futures or options trading during this period. But it also means that you should have funds available in subsequent periods for additional trading should you lose your entire outlay in a prior period. If you are doing well, you can increase your commitment in future periods by the amount you've gained in prior periods.

If you are not confident that gold will be moving in your favor, don't feel that you must always be in the market. Choose your times to commit funds to futures or options. And, of course, if your bearish at times—or perhaps you disagree with the fundamental bullish premise of this book—you can use these instruments to short the market and profit from a decline in price.

Recommendations for Some Typical Investors

Young couple with or without children: Begin buying gold coins according to your means. If all you can afford is 1 or 2 ounces once or twice a year, that's better than nothing. But, what ever you do, allocate some of your basic long-term savings to gold and add to your nest egg from year to year. If you invest in mutual funds, as many young couples do, make sure that between 10 and 30 percent of your mutual fund investment dollars are in a gold-oriented mutual fund.

Yuppies: Buy coins on a regular basis, perhaps 1 to 10 ounces every month or quarter. If you play the stock market, pick two, three, or four of the leading gold stocks for appreciation during the coming bull market in gold. Put at least 10 percent, and as much as 50 percent of your overall stock portfolio, in gold mining shares. Otherwise, put a similar percentage in one or two of the leading gold funds. If you're more intrepid, futures or options trading is fine—but don't speculate with money that you cannot afford to lose.

Double income, no kids (DINKs): You can afford to be more aggressive. After you have established basic positions in bullion and mining stocks or mutual funds, begin a program of careful speculation in futures or options. But first make sure you understand the market's fundamentals and technical picture—so that you are mindful of the best moments to trade and when to take profits.

Middle aged with kids: College is coming up. Unless you are in an upper income bracket, you've got to be more conservative in your savings and investment program. If you have not done so previously, begin a long-term coin buying program. If you already own stocks or mutual funds, make sure that from 10 to 30 percent of these assets are in gold related holdings.

Middle-aged, post-college: Consider yourself a DINK and follow the related guidelines. If you are saving for retirement, some of these funds should be in gold and/or gold stocks. If you are in the upper income brackets, you can consider speculating in futures and options, but never more than you can afford to lose.

Retired, middle income: You probably have a fixed income, perhaps it's interest sensitive since you've put some of your savings into money market accounts and the like, and possibly you have some long-term bonds or high-yield utility stocks or similar equities. Unfortunately, your holdings are very vulnerable to a sharp rise in inflation—but perhaps you don't have excess cash or savings to invest in gold bullion or coins. Still you could gain a little protection by purchasing some gold and/or gold mining equities and writing out-of-the money covered calls on a portion of these holdings to generate additional income.

Retired, wealthy: You are in the best position to take all of the preceding actions: Buy coins, invest in equities or mutual funds, and if you're so inclined, speculate in futures or options. In particular, remember that gold coins are an ideal way of passing wealth along to your heirs. Perhaps you might give gold coins regularly to your children and grandchildren. And, if you own bullion or coins, make sure your heirs know where they are stored and have access to your holdings.

Caveat Emptor

Gold investing has long been considered risky business. Nothing could be further from the truth. Wise investors use gold to reduce risk. And, those choosing to invest or speculate in gold equities, gold futures, or gold-related options need not take on any more risk than nongold investors or speculators in equities, futures, or options.

If gold investing has gotten bad press, it is because too many gold investors, lured by greed and the promise of big gains, have invested unwisely. In addition to the commonsense guidelines already enumerated, there are a number of "golden rules for gold investors," which can help you avoid the most common mistakes.

Golden Rules for Gold Investors

1. Do your homework. Don't invest in anything you don't understand.

2. Never follow the unsolicited trading advice of a broker or salesperson. Beware of any telephone salesperson making promises of big gains.

3. Never buy gold or other investments from a company you don't know well or can't thoroughly check out. In other words, always do business with a reputable broker or dealer.

4. If you prefer physical delivery, buy only bullion coins and only the better known brands.

5. Whether kept at home or in your own bank safe-deposit box, make sure your gold is fully insured, preferably by a policy which will cover the full value of your investment including any appreciation which may occur after the policy is in place.

6. If you are leaving bullion or coins in a storage account, make sure the gold is allocated to you and not commingled with the vendor's own holdings.

7. If you are leaving bullion or coins in a storage account, make sure it's insured and stored in a reputable depository.

8. Own bullion coins or bars before buying mutual funds or equities.

9. Own mutual funds or equities before speculating in futures or options.

10. Never buy a penny stock or exploration company as a gold play. Their prospects depend more on their company's success than on the gold price.

11. If you're trading stocks, futures, or options learn to read the charts—that is, become a technician—for clues to timing.

12. Never risk more than you can easily afford to lose when speculating in futures and options.

15

An Introduction to Technical Analysis

Introduction

Technical analysis is the art—some would say the science—of divining the future from the past. Technicians, or chartists as they are sometimes called, study the price history of gold, other commodities, equities, futures, options, or any other asset. They are looking for patterns that repeat themselves or offer pointers to the future price.

So many investors and traders, especially in the gold market, pay attention to technical signals that their collective expectations often become self-fulfilling. Technical trading signals for short periods of time, as a result, can become the driving force behind the movement in the metal's price. If for no other reason, every gold trader and investor should consult the charts.

During 1990 and 1991, much of the gold market's daily ups and downs were governed by technically inspired trading. In fact, one large trader representing a syndicate of wealthy Arabs made millions because they understood how other technically based traders would respond to their own buying and selling activities. They would sell, for example, at certain price levels, knowing that if those levels were broken, technical sell signals would result in widespread selling by others and sharply lower prices would follow. Then, the Arab syndicate would buy back its original position at a profit and wait for another opportunity to snooker the market.

While fundamental analysis may help us decide whether or not to invest in gold with a medium- to long-term time horizon, technical analysis helps us pick the right moment to invest and the right time to take profits. If you're interested in trading with a short-term orientation, technical analysis is indispensable. Moreover, an educated and informed market participant must know what the technical situation is at any given time—and how others who follow the charts may react to any change in the price.

There are several methods of technical analysis. Just as you should not be wed entirely to either fundamental analysis or technical analysis, so you also should not restrict yourself exclusively to any one method of technical analysis. Many technicians believe in the "rule of multiple techniques," that is, looking for confirmation of a prospective price move from several different technical signals—and this is a methodology I wholly endorse.

For example, if a simple *high-low-close* bar chart points to a pending change in the direction of gold prices, while other technical tools fail to indicate the same prospective price change, it may be best to be cautious and disregard the bar chart for the time being. In addition to different techniques of technical analysis, you should also look for confirmation in different but related markets, such as gold equities or options, or in gold prices denominated in different currencies such as Japanese yen or Swiss francs.

This chapter will teach you the basic tools of the trade, so that you can do your own technical analysis, if you so choose, or better understand the technical indicators and analysis that may be published in your favorite investment newsletters.

Bar Charts

Technical analysis generally begins with the construction of charts and graphs which provide a visual picture of the market. The *daily high-low-close* bar chart is one of the most popular and certainly one of the simplest forms of charting. Figure 15.1, which represents 17 days of gold futures trading on COMEX, is an example of a daily high-low-close chart. Similar charts can be constructed for individual equities or even mutual funds. The vertical line for each trading day shows the full price range for that day from the lowest point to the highest price, while the small horizontal line intersecting the vertical bar indicates the closing or settlement price for the day.

Simply looking at a bar chart will give you a quick picture of the direction of the market as well as how volatile it is—that is, how wide the

Figure 15.1. Daily high-low-close bar chart.

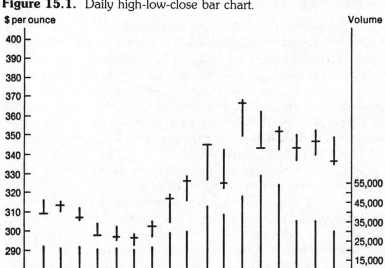

trading range is on both an intraday basis as well as over a period of days, weeks, or months depending on the length of time charted. Bar charts can, and should, be plotted using weekly and even monthly data for longer time intervals.

Many technicians will also plot on the same chart the daily (weekly or monthly) trading volume—in this case, the number of futures contracts traded each day—by using a different vertical scale, as I have done along the bottom right of Fig. 15.1. Analysts often impute more importance to particular price signals if they occur with a rise in trading volume.

Many technicians will tell you that there is nothing like drawing their own charts to get a real feel for a market. All you need is ordinary graph paper. If you're plotting a daily chart, let each line or box along the horizontal axis equal one day. Along the vertical axis, draw a price scale that's wide enough to incorporate the recent trading range plus some. Then, using the price data for COMEX gold futures contracts (use the nearby active month) from your daily newspaper or *The Wall Street Journal*, you can begin to plot each day's price performance.

Alternatively, you can subscribe to one of the many charting services covering commodity futures and/or equity markets. For computer users, there are also a number of software packages and on-line data services that facilitate the creation of technical charts.

Spotting Trends

Now that you have constructed a bar chart for the past few weeks or months, you are ready to begin analyzing. The first thing to look for is a price trend—a persistent upward or downward movement in prices over a period of time. If a quick glance at the chart shows either an uptrend or a downtrend, take a ruler and connect the highest point at the beginning of the move with the highest point at the end of the move. Then put your pencil on the lowest point at the beginning of the move and draw a second line connecting the lowest point at the beginning, or the trend, to the lowest point at the end of the trend.

If your two lines are roughly parallel, as they are in Fig. 15.2, then you have drawn an upward or downward sloping *channel*. Once defined, an upward or downward sloping channel is an excellent guide to where futures traders should place stop orders (see Chap. 12), since the upper line defines resistance and the lower line defines support, either of which, if pierced, could be followed by a further sharp move out of the channel. If the lines are not parallel, then perhaps you've uncovered another sort of chart formation, possibly a triangle, rectangle, flag, or pennant—all of which I'll review later in this chapter.

Figure 15.2. Bar chart with channel.

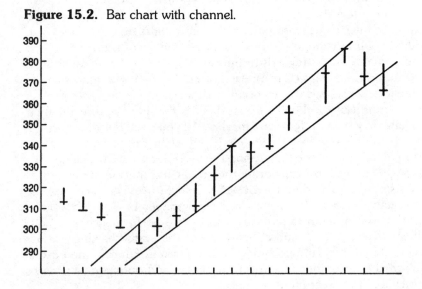

Minor Trends and Key Reversals

Channels which endure for several weeks, months, or years are considered major trends. Within these major trends, there often will be what technicians call *minor trends* which zigzag within the major channel. Even if the market is not in a noticeable major trend, minor trends may still be detectable. Figure 15.3 shows minor trends within major trends on a weekly high-low-close chart.

One thing a chartist looks for is a *key reversal* of a trend. This occurs after prices move in one direction—say lower—over a period of time, then in one single trading day, a new low for the move is established before prices turn higher and close up for the day. A key reversal, as its name suggests, could represent the start of a new trend. If the new high price at the close of a key reversal day is higher than the previous trading day's high, the day is called an *outside day*—and this often indicates that the market direction may be changing. If the new high is higher than the previous day's settlement or closing price, but below the previous day's high, the day is called an *inside day*—and this is a weaker, less significant signal.

Figure 15.3. Major and minor trend lines.

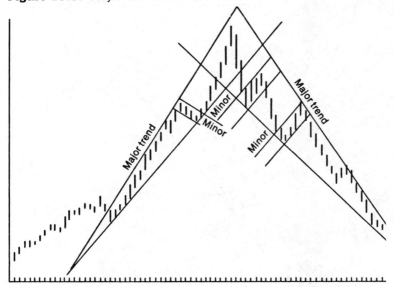

The most significant key reversal signal occurs when the highs and lows for a particular trading day not only exceed the prior day's trading range and the close is above the prior day's close, making it an outside day, but the price move also breaks through the channel. Such a pattern is illustrated in Fig. 15.4.

Bar Chart Formations—
Head and Shoulders

There are a variety of chart formations—in addition to trend lines and channels—that excite technicians because they are reliable precursors of the market. One of the classic patterns is the *head and shoulders* formation. As its name suggests, it vaguely resembles a pair of shrugged shoulders separated by a man's head. A head and shoulders formation indicates that the market's momentum has been broken and a reversal may be at hand. Figure 15.5 depicts a head-and-shoulders pattern that is signaling an end to an upward trend in price. If the pattern were turned upside down, it would be known as a *reverse head and shoulders*—and it would be signaling the possible end of a downtrend.

Head and shoulders formations are characterized by a series of three price moves, with the initial and final moves less extreme than the middle move. In charting such a series of moves, you should first mark out

Figure 15.4. Key reversal.

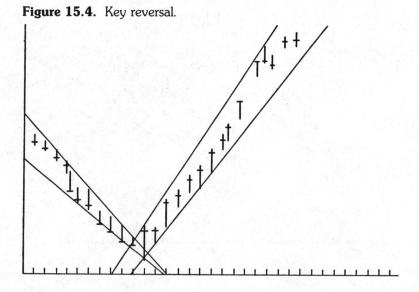

[handwritten notes at top: Tech. signals end of an up trend. Reverse H&S signals ewl to downtrend.]

Figure 15.5. Head and shoulders.

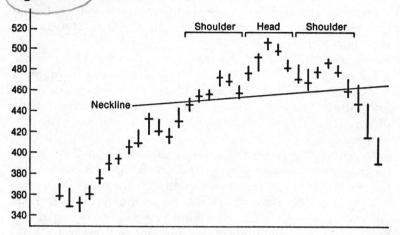

channel lines on a high-low-close bar chart to help determine whether you have a true head and shoulders formation. Imagine the first price rally as the left arm leading up to the shoulder, the second price rally leading from the shoulder to the top of the head, and the third rally, a minor one, leading from the neckline back up to the top of the right shoulder. The shoulder top must be below the top of the head (but may be either higher or lower than the left shoulder top) to qualify as a legitimate head and shoulders formation.

Next, draw a *neckline* across the chart connecting the low points of each shoulder (where the shoulders and the head come together). A true head and shoulders will show prices dropping through the neckline to form the right arm. In many cases when the price does break down through the neckline, it foretells a further steep price decline. Many technicians believe that this subsequent decline should equal the distance from the top of the head to the neckline.

Rectangles, Triangles, Pennants, and Flags

Looking at a high-low-close bar chart, you may see other familiar geometric patterns aside from parallel channels and head and shoulders formations. Technicians refer to these formations as rectangles, triangles, pennants, and flags. As often as not, they are merely pauses interrupting a trend rather than an indication that the market is changing direction. These formations result from congestion in trading, that is, a period when prices appear to be hovering around one level. If these formations persist for lengthy periods, the next move—up or down—may be dramatic. Nevertheless, identifying these patterns can provide useful clues in planning a short-term trading strategy.

A *rectangle* is an extended horizontal drift, with the top of the rectangle forming a resistance level and the bottom of the rectangle forming a support line, as shown in Fig. 15.6. The ultimate breakout may be either up or down. But, when it does occur, many technicians believe that the extent of the subsequent move will equal the distance between the support and resistance lines.

Triangles are another pattern that technicians look for in their charts. These come in three varieties: symmetrical, ascending, and descending. As can be seen in Fig. 15.7, a *symmetrical triangle* is one where the top is a downtrending resistance line and the bottom is an uptrending support line. An *ascending triangle* has an uptrending resistance line along the top but a horizontal support line along the bottom. A *descending triangle* has a downtrending support line along the bottom and a horizontal resistance line along the top.

Rarely will a triangle be perfect—but, remember, when you spot one forming, it usually does not indicate a change in the market's basic trend or direction. A symmetrical triangle, however, can be helpful in timing a trade. Prices usually trade in an increasingly narrow range until the point at which the support and resistance lines intersect. Then technicians will expect a breakout—usually but not always—in the direction of the longer-term trend.

Figure 15.6. Rectangle.

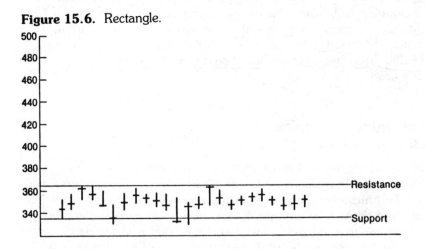

Figure 15.7. Triangles.

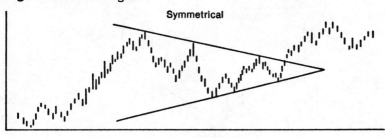

Symmetrical

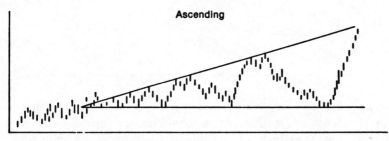

Ascending

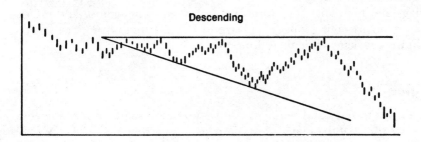

Descending

A flag or pennant is a chart formation that looks roughly like a rectangle or triangle drawn around a price move. The rectangular formation is a *flag*, the triangular one is a *pennant*. But unlike the rectangle and triangle patterns, which are horizontal, flags and pennants are either ascending or descending. If the flag or pennant is sloping downward, with its highest point on the left, this is considered a bull formation—evidence of a temporary downtrend that constitutes a break in a continuing uptrend. A bull flag is illustrated in Fig. 15.8.

If the flag or pennant is sloping upward, with its low point on the left, then it is a bear formation—evidence of a temporary uptrend that constitutes a break in a continuing uptrend. To be a true flag or pennant, the

Figure 15.8. Bull flag formation.

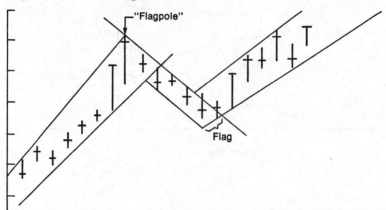

formation must have a *flagpole* formed by a sharp move in one direction over a short time span. The flagpole for a bull flag or pennant is a spurt in the price that makes up the left-hand side of the formation. The flagpole for a bear flag or pennant is a drop in price followed by a rising formation.

Flags and pennants are short-term trends moving against, and interrupting the prevailing longer-term trend. They do not represent a reversal in the market's basic direction.

Slopes

In contrast to flags and pennants, *slopes* go in the same direction as the previous trend of the market but often are precursors of a market reversal. Slopes occur after a steep move in one direction or the other. While the trend of a slope is unchanged from the market's previous direction, the movement is not as rapid, as illustrated in Fig. 15.9. Technical analysts believe that a slope indicates an impending reversal. It occurs because the market's move is losing momentum and suggests an overbought or oversold condition.

In an oversold market, there are few holders of gold willing to sell at the current price level. Consequently, prices are likely to rise in order to attract new sellers. In an overbought market, there are few new buyers willing to pay a higher price so that prices are likely to fall in order to attract new buyers. When prices break out of a slope and reverse the previous trend, the price often rises or falls beyond the starting point of the slope and continue moving until they reach the market's prior area of price congestion.

Figure 15.9. Slopes.

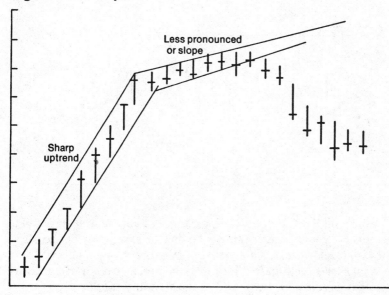

Double Tops and Bottoms

Occasionally, when the price of gold registers a new high for a move (whether you're looking at a short-term daily chart covering a period of a few months or a long-term monthly bar chart extending over many years), falls back, and then moves back to the vicinity of the previous high point—but fails to break into still higher territory and, instead, drops back again, technical analysts refer to this as a *double top* formation. The mirror image of this is known as a *double bottom*. Double tops and double bottoms are indications that the market does not have enough fundamental impetus to continue its previous trend. In other words, they signal a market that has run out of steam. Once in a while, markets may even try a third time to break through resistance or support—forming, respectively, a *triple top* or *triple bottom* formation. This is an even stronger indication that the previous extremes were unsustainable and that the price is probably in the process of reversing.

Gaps

Generally, when you look at a daily price chart extending over several months, you will note that each day's trading activity overlaps the prior

Figure 15.10. Double top.

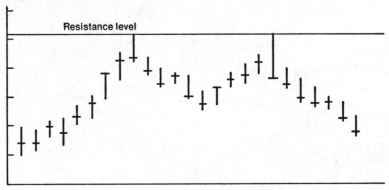

day's trading range. When the trading ranges of consecutive days fail to overlap, this creates a pattern known to chartists as *gaps*. Figure 15.11 illustrates what is known as a *breakaway gap*—that is, one that precedes a change in market direction. In addition to the breakaway variety, gaps are also classified as *common, midway* or *runaway,* and *exhaustion.*

The common gap is the most frequent, though least significant, of these formations. The common gap usually occurs in a trendless market and is often *filled* in the next few trading days—that is, prices trade in subsequent sessions within the range of the gap itself. Breakaway gaps, as already noted, are significant because they often signal the beginning of a new trend. Unlike common gaps, breakaway gaps do not usually get filled

Figure 15.11. Breakaway gap.

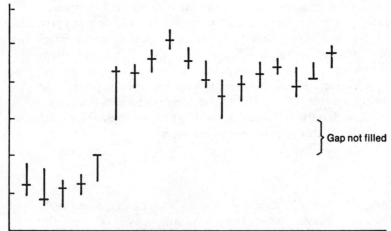

in subsequent sessions but, instead, serve as a support level when the new trend is up, or resistance zone when the new trend is down. If what looks like a breakaway gap does get filled in subsequent sessions, it suggests that it was a false signal and that a reversal has probably not occurred.

Midway or runaway gaps occur, as the name suggests, in the middle of a price move and, hence, are generally not significant indicators. Midway gaps may or may not be filled in subsequent trading sessions. In contrast, an exhaustion gap—as depicted in Fig. 15.12—is often an indicator that a long-prevailing market trend is in the process of reversing. As its name implies, it is indicative of a market which is exhausted and unable to continue the prevailing price trend. If you notice a gap pattern after a long-term uptrend or downtrend, watch out. It may be an exhaustion gap presaging a reversal. Figure 15.12 pictures the gold market in January

Figure 15.12. Exhaustion gap.

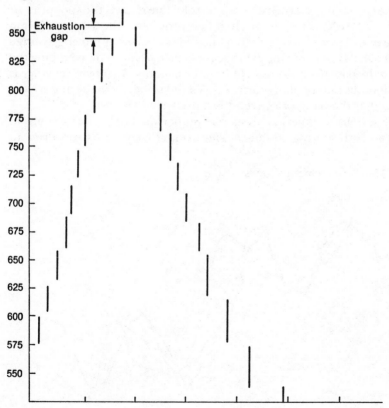

1980—one of the best examples of an exhaustion gap—when the market lurched to more than $850 an ounce before reversing.

At times, midway gaps and exhaustion gaps are easily misinterpreted or confused. It may take a day or two to figure out which is which—but when the subsequent trading sessions confirm that the trend is continuing or has been reversed, the technical trader will know what to do.

Moving Averages

The examination of a high-low-close bar chart (whether daily, weekly, or monthly) for significant price formations is perhaps the simplest and most popular form of technical analysis. But it is by no means the only form of charting. Another popular, but somewhat more complex tool of the technician's trade is the construction of *moving averages*. A moving average chart compares the average price of gold (or some other asset) over the past 5, 30, or even 200 days with the current price. Figure 15.13 illustrates a moving average chart. The solid line depicts the spot price of gold on COMEX, while the dashed line represents the 10-day moving average of this price and the dotted line shows the 20-day moving average price. (Each day, the moving average is calculated simply by averaging the prices of the past 10 or 20 days.) One of the benefits of a moving average is that it smooths out the short-term wiggles and squiggles in the underlying price so that the basic price trend is more readily visible.

Many serious technical analysts rely on personal computer systems to quickly and efficiently generate moving average charts and to experiment

Figure 15.13. Moving averages.

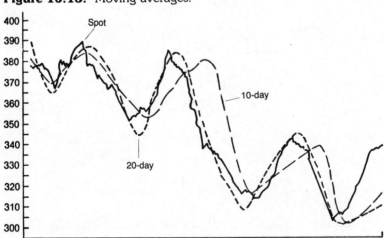

with a variety of moving average time periods. Others may calculate and plot their moving average charts by hand and/or subscribe to one of the popular chart services which publish weekly updates.

Technical analysts look for points where two lines cross. For example, if the spot price crosses the 200-day moving average price, many analysts believe that this may signify a change in market direction. During the past few years, the 200-day moving average price, has been a popular indicator among gold market chartists. In addition, these analysts define the 200-day moving average as a resistance level (if the spot price is below the long-term average) or a support level (if the spot price is above the long-term average). Longer-term moving averages are called *trend lines*—and, up to a point, the longer the time period of the trend line, the more significant it is as an indicator.

Some technicians use weighted moving averages, preferring to assign more importance to recent prices and less importance to prices in the more distant past. One approach in calculating a 10-day weighted average, for example, is to assign a weight of 10 to the prior day's value (that is,

Figure 15.14.

SOURCE: First Boston Canada Limited.

Figure 15.15. Five-day oscillator and moving average price.

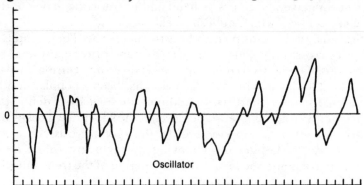

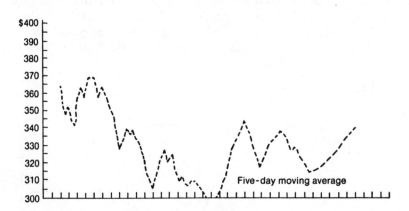

multiply yesterday's price by 10), assign a weight of 9 to the price two days earlier, a weight of 8 to the price three days earlier, and so on. Once you have multiplied each day's price by its weight, divide the total by the sum of the weights (in this case, 55) to get the weighted moving average. Proponents of this technique argue that the most recent price data is more representative of the current market situation but the inclusion of older data still helps smooth out the picture, making the market's direction more apparent. Like any system, moving averages may give you an indication of the market's direction, but in the end, there is no replacement for common sense.

Oscillators

Analysts are often interested in the velocity of, and rate of change in, the movement in prices. *Net change oscillators* are standard measures of how

fast prices are changing. Daily net change oscillators may be easily constructed plotting the net change in price from one day to the next—that is,
the latest day's closing price minus the prior day's closing price. For
example, if today's settlement price is $370 an ounce and yesterday's price
was $368, your first plot point on the chart would be +2. Figure 15.15
shows a five-day net change oscillator, which plots the net change between
each day's closing price and the price five days earlier.

Net change oscillators are often helpful in spotting potential changes in
the underlying trend. If a price rise is slowing, for instance, it may indicate
that the upswing is losing momentum and will soon come to an end.

Point and Figure Charts

Some technical analysts prefer *point and figure charts* to the high-low-
close charts, moving averages, and oscillators that have been discussed.
This technique of charting can help discern changes in the direction of a
market—whether you are analyzing gold bullion, mining equities, or any
other asset. At times, point and figure charts also may be helpful in
predicting the extent of prospective price changes.

These charts most often are based on intraday prices—something the
average investor is not likely to have ready access to—but may also be
constructed using the end-of-day settlement or closing prices. Many day
traders rely on point and figure charts, updating there graphs frequently

Figure 15.16. Point and figure chart.

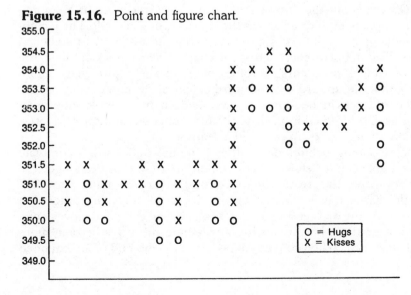

during the course of the day. Serious chartists will often use a computer with access to real-time price data to plot these charts on a continuous basis on their computer screen. But, even if you lack computer charting facilities, you can still benefit from point and figure charts by subscribing to one of the weekly chart services and updating the printed charts by hand at the close of each trading day, just as you might update your high-low-close bar charts, moving average charts, and oscillators, if you subscribe to such a service.

The technician looks to point and figure charts for signs of price congestion—periods of low volatility with very little change in price, when there appears to be a good balance between buyers and sellers around current price levels. A bar chart may give similar indications when the length of each bar (whether it represents a day, a week, or a month) is short and when consecutive bars over an extended period of time all fall in a narrow range. As noted earlier, this pattern is a rectangle formation.

Figure 15.16 shows a point and figure chart which plots each 50-cent movement in the price of gold as an X for up moves or an O for down moves. Chartists often refer to the down moves as *hugs* and the up moves as *kisses*. Each time the price moves by the required 50-cent interval another X or O is added to the chart. (These charts can be constructed using any minimum price interval from 10 cents to a dollar or more.) As long as the price is rising, the X marks are stacked one above the other. A new column begins only after a 50-cent reversal has occurred—and then the O marks are placed below each other until the market again reverses by the required 50-cent interval.

Figure 15.16 indicates a period of congestion where the columns of X's and O's are about the same length until there is a series of X's going straight up, about midway across the chart starting at $350. The technician looking at a point and figure chart concentrates on the number of blocks filled in horizontally across the chart. When a break out from the area of congestion occurs, devotees of point and figure charts often believe that the upward or downward extent of the move will equal the number of blocks in the prior sideways trend. In this example, nine boxes across have been filled in prior to the breakout—so the projected move should be nine blocks up or $4.50 an ounce.

The reasoning behind this is that potential trades will accumulate unfilled above and below the congestion area—so that the longer the congestion area, the greater number of trades that are waiting to be filled once the market moves into new territory. Generally speaking, congestion occurs when the market stabilizes after making an extended move in one direction or the other, as buying and selling pressures become more evenly matched. When congestion occurs at the low end of an extended downtrend, the breakout is likely to be toward the upside. Conversely, a breakout from an area of congestion following a long-term uptrend is likely to be toward the downside.

Point and figure charts, in my view, have a place in the technician's tool box—but the rule of multiple techniques cautions against relying entirely on any single methodology.

Contrary Opinion

Not all technical tools rely on price statistics. One of the most important nonprice indicators is contrary opinion. If the consensus view of gold market prospects were always right, trading and investing would be easy. But, in fact, the majority view often seems to be wrong—and this is the basis of contrary opinion.

The contrarian approach is based upon the notion that the current market price already reflects the collective thinking of all the market participants. If most people are bullish, the price already reflects this. Taking an extreme view, if everybody was already extremely bullish on gold, all potential buyers would have already bought—and the price would be at its highest possible level since there would be no new buyers to push it still higher. Therefore, the contrarian would predict an imminent decline in the price.

There are a number of publications and technical services which survey the views of commodity analysts and newsletter writers on a regular basis in order to gauge the percentage of analysts that are bullish or bearish. When most of those surveyed are bullish, chances are that the market is at or near an overbought position. When most are bearish, the market is probably oversold. In either case, technicians would expect a market reversal before too long.

Warehouse Stocks

Most holders of gold around the world—investors, dealers, refiners, and industrial users—do not reveal the extent of their inventories. But statistics on the quantity of gold bullion held in exchange-related warehouses, which may be delivered against futures contracts, is available daily, from the Commodity Exchange, Inc. in New York.

At times, changes in the level of COMEX-related warehouse stocks of gold will be of great interest to technicians. A large increase in the supply of deliverable gold over a short time span is generally viewed as a bearish indicator. Deliverable supplies may be rising, for example, because of weaker demand from industrial users or because of rising output from producers or scrap refiners. In contrast, a drop in deliverable supplies of gold held in exchange-related warehouses may indicate rising demand from commercial interests or from investors wishing physical delivery; falling warehouse stocks are viewed as a bullish signal.

In all reality, changes in COMEX stocks often reflect other factors entirely that have little or no bearing on the price—factors such as shifts in dealer or commercial inventories from one location to another or arbitrage activities by major bullion houses. Nevertheless, the rise and fall in warehouse stocks are generally viewed as indicators so that they have, at the very least, an important psychological impact on the market.

Open Interest

Another important statistic for the technician is *open interest*. This is the number of outstanding futures contracts which have not been offset or liquidated, either by opposite transactions or by delivery of the underlying asset. Rising open interest, coupled with rising prices, would be a technical signal that there are new buyers entering the gold futures market. Rising open interest, coincidental with falling prices, suggests that there are new sellers entering the market.

A fall in open interest, accompanying a fall in prices, indicates that holders of long positions are liquidating their contracts, either to take existing profits or avoid further losses. Finally, declining open interest, occurring in tandem with rising prices, is a sign that those who had previously sold short, that is, entered into contracts to deliver gold, are buying back those contracts because they anticipate higher prices or are satisfied with any profits that have already accrued to their positions.

Open interest and warehouse stocks are statistics relating to futures markets. Comparable data are not available or relevant to the technical analysis of equities, or most other assets.

Commitment of Traders

Once every month, the Commodity Futures Trading Commission, the U.S. government agency responsible for regulating futures markets, issues a *commitment of traders report* detailing the number of positions— short and long—held by hedgers, large speculators, and small speculators. Hedgers—commercial firms that use gold in the course of their

business, such as jewelry manufacturers, refiners, miners, and dealers—
are important participants in gold futures markets. But their trading
activities are usually governed by the requirements of their business.

Large and small speculators, on the other hand, are trading gold
futures only to profit from an expected change in the metal's price.
Contrarians might use commitment of traders reports for evidence of a
consensus about price prospects. A large number of speculators holding
long positions might indicate an overbought market ready for a correction, while a large number of short positions among speculators might
suggest that the market is oversold.

Market Volume

Each day, the Commodity Exchange, Inc. publishes data on daily trading
volume indicating the total number of contracts traded. Similar statistics
are available for other gold futures exchanges around the world but are
not readily available to the average investor or speculator. COMEX
volume, however, is published along with futures prices in many daily
newspapers as well as in *The Wall Street Journal* and *Investors Daily*.
Equity market volume for individual stocks is also reported daily in the
stock tables of your newspaper.

A jump in volume generally indicates that a rising number of speculators or investors were active in the market. High volume, coupled with
rising prices, is an indication that many new buyers were entering the
market. Heavy volume, coupled with falling prices, suggests that speculators were liquidating long positions, or entering into short positions in
expectation of a decline in the price of gold. Low volume, regardless of
the market's direction, signifies the absence of speculators and investors.
Generally, key reversals in the various chart formations, and moving
averages discussed earlier in this chapter, have more significance when
they coincide with high volume on COMEX.

Summary

Whether you are a long-term investor or a short-term trader, whether
your interest in gold bullion, mining equities, futures, or options on any
of these various gold-related assets, technical analysis has its place along-
side fundamental analysis as a guide to prospective price moves and
market timing. But technical analysis is as much an art as it may be a
science—so that success depends, in part, on the skill and experience of
the analyst.

Most of the examples discussed in this chapter rely upon futures market prices and related data. Economists argue that futures markets serve as arenas for efficient price discovery because they are true auction markets where a multitude of buyers and sellers come together. In the case of the Commodity Exchange, Inc., the world's principal gold futures market, buyers and sellers—most often operating through intermediaries—represent many of the major players in the world of gold. So that the price patterns that emerge from this beehive of activity are arguably the most significant price data available to the technical analyst.

The rule of multiple techniques cautions the analyst not to rely on any one system or tool of technical analysis. As an extension of this rule, it makes sense not to rely solely on fundamentals—trends in gold supply and demand—for insight into the metal's future. At the very least, the investor needs to look at the daily high-low-close bar chart for a sense of where gold has been trading and for clues to where it may be heading.

In addition to looking for the significant chart formations discussed—head and shoulders, rectangles, triangles, and double tops or bottoms, for example—it is wise to be familiar with the popular moving averages, such as the 200-day moving average, because the crossover points (where the spot price crosses the moving average) often signifies a possible breakout. If you are trading or investing in gold mining stocks, look at the chart patterns for a number of actively traded gold equities (like Homestake, American Barrick, and ASA) and for the indexes representing baskets of gold equities. Even if your not investing in gold stocks, look at the equity market bar charts and moving averages for confirmation of the patterns that you may be seeing in other markets. Indeed, the gold equities often lead the bullion market so that the charts on gold mining company stock prices can be especially relevant to your decision making.

Many of the other indicators in the technician's toolbox—such as oscillators, commitment of traders reports, open interest, volume and contrary opinion—can also add to your understanding of the market and its prospective course. The successful investor is usually the best informed—and this means being aware of the complete technical picture as well as the fundamentals of supply and demand.

A Glossary of Gold and Gold Investment Terms

Note: Throughout this glossary, words or phrases enclosed in quotation marks are further explained under their own headings.

Actuals: This refers to the actual metal as opposed to futures and forward contracts. *See also* Physicals.

Adit: A tunnel driven horizontally into a mountain or hillside in order to access mineralization for exploration or mining.

Allocated Gold: Gold that is stored in a bank or bullion depository in a segregated account belonging to a specific owner. *See also* Unallocated gold.

Alloy: A mixture of metals. Because it is extremely soft, gold is often alloyed with small amounts of other metals, particularly silver, platinum, palladium, copper, nickel, or zinc. Alloys of gold are often used for coins and jewelry. Alloying gold with other metals may also be used for affecting the color, especially of jewelry.

Alluvial Gold: Small particles or nuggets of gold formed by the weathering and erosion of gold-bearing rocks and often deposited downstream by rivers and streams. Also known as "placer" gold, it is often mined by panning or dredging of river edges or beds.

American Depository Receipt (ADR): Certificates issued by American banks representing ownership of foreign securities to simplify investment by Americans in foreign stocks. The issuing bank holds the actual security. ADRs allow investors to own foreign stocks—especially Australian and South African mining stocks—without having to worry about exchange rates, trading in distant time zones, and delivery of foreign stock certificates, because the ADRs are priced in U.S. dollars and trade on U.S. stock exchanges or over-the-counter markets.

Apothecaries' Weight: Literally, the weighing system used by pharmacists. Gold and other precious metals are traditionally weighed in "troy ounces" which are units of the apothecary system. One troy ounce equals 31.1035 grams, while a standard or avoirdupois ounce equals 28.349 grams.

Approved Refiner: A commercial refiner whose branded bars are accepted for "good delivery" by certain market organizations. The "London Gold Bullion Association" and the "Commodity Exchange, Inc.," for example, each have their own lists of approved refiners and good delivery bars.

Arbitrage: The simultaneous buying and selling of gold (or other commodities and assets) in two different markets, exchanges, or locations in order to profit from small differences in price. Arbitrage may be done between physical and futures markets, between different physical markets (such as London and New York), or between different delivery months in the same futures market. *See also* Spread and Straddle.

Ask: The price sought by the seller of gold (or other commodities and investments).

Assay: A chemical or physical analysis of ore, scrap, alloys, jewelry, bars, or other forms of gold-containing materials in order to determine the exact gold content and the presence of other minerals.

At-the-Money: An option market term describing the price point when the option "strike price" and the current market price of the underlying asset are the same.

Au: The chemical symbol for gold originating with the Latin word aurum which means shining dawn, after the goddess of the dawn, Aurora.

Aureus: An ancient Roman gold coin.

Australian Nugget: A range of 0.9999 fine (24 karat) gold coins issued by the Perth Mint in a variety of sizes. Originally, the coins were minted in one-ounce, half-ounce, quarter-ounce, and tenth-ounce units. The coins, at first, featured the design of famous gold nuggets on their "reverse" side but in 1990 this was replaced with the imprint of a kangaroo. In 1991, two-ounce, ten-ounce, and kilogram units were introduced.

Austrian Corona: This coin, minted by the Austrian National Mint, is a "restrike" of the old Austrian 100-Corona which was the "legal tender" circulating coin in 1915. It bears the image of Emperor Franz Josef I on the "obverse" and the Imperial double-headed eagle on the "reverse." With a "fineness" of 0.9000 (21.6 karat) and a gross weight of 1.0891 ounces, it contains 0.9802 troy ounces of fine gold, making price calculations awkward.

Bear: Someone who believes that the price of gold will fall.

Bear Market: A market characterized by a persistent and long-lasting downtrend in price.

Bear Spread: An options trading strategy combining the purchase of one option and the sale of another with a different strike price in order to profit from an expected decline in the underlying price of gold.

Beta: A statistical measure of the amount of variation or volatility between the prices of different investment assets. Gold and gold mining stocks have a high beta in relation to ordinary equities and bonds. In other words, gold prices move differently than the prices of other investment assets.

Bid: The price a potential buyer is willing to pay for gold (or other commodities or investments).

Britannia: A "bullion coin" issued since 1987 by the British Royal Mint. Minted in one-ounce, half-ounce, quarter-ounce, and tenth-ounce weights, these legal tender coins are 0.9167 fine (22 karat).

British Sovereign: For centuries, this gold coin, bearing the image of the reigning sovereign, was the circulating currency of the United Kingdom. After the suspension of the gold standard in 1914, the Royal Mint has continued striking new Sovereigns as investment coins with a price based upon gold content. The coin is 0.9167 fine (22 karat) and contains 0.24 troy ounces of fine gold.

Bull: Someone who believes that the price of gold will rise.

Bull Market: A market characterized by a persistent and long-lasting uptrend in price.

Bull Spread: An options trading strategy combining the purchase of one option and the sale of another with a different strike price in order to profit from an expected rise in the underlying price of gold.

Bullion: Refined bars or "ingots" of gold (or silver), typically of high purity, which are traded, held by central banks and investors, and used as the raw material in jewelry fabrication and other industrial applications requiring gold.

Bullion Coin: A coin, the value of which is based on its gold content. These coins are minted as gold investment products and trade at a small, stable premium above the current market price of gold. In contrast, "numismatic coins" are collected for their scarcity value and trade at large and variable premiums above their gold content value. The major bullion coins are the South African "Krugerrand," the American "Eagle," the Canadian "Maple Leaf," the "Australian Nugget," and the Austrian "Philharmonic."

By-Product: A mineral or metal of secondary importance that is mined or refined along with another mineral or metal. For example, gold is often produced as a by-product of copper mines, and silver is often produced as a by-product of gold mines.

Call or Call Option: A contract giving the buyer the right, but not the obligation, to purchase bullion, equities, or futures contracts at a specified price (the "strike price") on or before a specified date. The seller or grantor of the option is obligated to deliver the underlying asset if requested by the buyer. Upon entering into an options contract the buyer pays the seller a fee or "premium" for the right to make the subsequent purchase.

Carat: The British spelling of "karat."

Carry: The cost of holding a gold (or some other commodity) futures contract equal to the premium of futures prices over the current or "spot" price. In the gold futures markets, this cost—representing the higher price for future delivery—is called the "contango."

Carrying Charges: The cost of storing gold bullion in a depository or warehouse including insurance fees and interest expenses associated with full financing of the bullion purchase.

Cash Production Cost: The cost of mining an ounce of gold generally including milling, refining, and other direct production costs, but usually excluding taxes, depreciation, financing, marketing, and other indirect expenses. The exact definition may vary from one mining company to another.

Centenario: A Mexican gold bullion coin with a face value of 50 pesos (also known as a 50-peso coin) and a gold content of 1.2057 troy ounces. These coins are 0.9000 fine (21.6 karat). Currently minted coins are "restrikes" dated 1947.

CFTC: *See* Commodity Futures Trading Commission.

Chervonetz: A gold bullion coin minted by the former Soviet Union. With a face value of 10 rubles, the coin is 0.9000 fine (21.6 karat) and contains 0.2489 troy ounces of gold.

Chartist: *See* Technical Analyst.

Chop or Chop Mark: A stamp used by the Chinese as a trademark to designate the weight and fineness of gold bars. The term has entered the jargon of the gold trade around the world and may often refer to the brand name of the refiner who produced the bar.

Chuk Kam: The Chinese phrase for pure gold, this refers to 0.990 fine investment-grade jewelry popular in Hong Kong and Mainland China. Chuk kam jewelry typically trades at a 10 to 15 percent premium over its gold content value.

Clearinghouse: An independent association responsible for matching up the buyers and sellers of futures contracts on commodity futures exchanges. The clearinghouse for "COMEX," the principal gold futures exchange, is the Commodity Clearing Association that is owned by the exchange's clearing member firms. The clearinghouse and its members guarantee every contract traded on the exchange and is responsible for collecting margin payments from all trading and brokerage firms doing business on the exchange. The clearinghouse assures the integrity and credibility of the exchange.

COMEX: *See* Commodity Exchange, Inc.

Commemorative: A coin issued to honor individuals or historic events. Usually, minted in limited quantities and sold at a significant premium over their gold (or silver) content value, as in the case of U.S. modern-issue commemoratives which are legal tender and carry a face value well below their metal value.

Commodity Exchange, Inc. The world's largest and most influential gold futures exchange which trades contracts representing future delivery of 100 ounces of gold. Known as COMEX, the exchange also trades silver, copper, and aluminum, as well as options on gold futures contracts.

Commodity Futures Trading Commission: The U.S. government agency charged with supervising and regulating futures exchanges in the United States.

Concentrate: Mine ore or other precious metals material which has been treated to remove certain unwanted constituents prior to final recovery of the contained metal.

Contango: Originally a British term used on the London Stock Exchange, and later the London Metal Exchange, to describe the premium paid by the buyer of an equity or commodity to postpone transfer and payment to the next day, contango today refers to the relationship between the current or "spot" price of gold and the higher price for future or forward delivery. The contango, or premium, for future delivery always approximates the cost of "carry," which is the cost of storing, insuring, and financing a physical bullion position less the "gold lease rate." Any discrepancy between the contango and the cost of carry minus the gold lease rate results in "arbitrage" by large bullion-dealing firms between the physical and futures markets.

Contract: A legally binding agreement to buy or sell a specified quantity of gold (or other commodities) at a contracted price and time in the future. Traders on futures exchanges are not actually dealing in the underlying commodity but are entering into contracts to make or take delivery in the future. Each gold contract on COMEX, for example, represents future delivery of 100 ounces of 0.995 fine gold at an exchange-approved warehouse location and in "good delivery" form.

Contract Month: The month in which a given commodity futures contract, unless previously liquidated, becomes deliverable.

Covered Option: If the writer or seller of an option on gold bullion, equities, or futures owns the underlying asset—and, therefore, can make delivery if required—the option is covered. In contrast, a "naked option" is one in which the underlying asset is not owned by the seller.

Cyanidation or Cyanide Process: The process of extracting precious metals from mine ore and scrap material using an oxygen-rich cyanide solution.

Day Order: Orders to buy or sell a commodity futures contract that expires at the end of the day's trading. If not filled during the course of the day, these orders are automatically withdrawn.

Day Trader: A commodity trader, usually on the floor of an exchange, who takes positions and liquidates them prior to the close of the same trading day.

Delivery: The transfer of ownership of gold (or other commodities) from one party to another; in gold futures markets, the tender of actual "bullion" against a "short" position in futures during the period allowed by the futures "contract." Delivery does not necessarily involve the physical movement of gold but is often accomplished through the transfer of a "warehouse receipt" indicating the quantity, brand, location, and serial numbers of the transferred bars.

Delivery Date: The specified time when a commodity, such as gold, must be delivered to fulfill a "futures contract."

Delivery Months: Months designated by a commodity futures exchange as times when "delivery notices" may be given. On "COMEX," the delivery months are February, April, June, August, October, and December.

Delivery Notice: The notice issued by the holders of short futures contracts of the time and place at which they will deliver physical gold. Delivery must always be made at an exchange-approved depository.

Delivery Period: The designated period during which holders of short futures contracts may give notice of their intention to deliver the actual gold. On "COMEX," for example, the deliver period begins two days after the last trading day of the previous month and extends one day beyond the "delivery month." Delivery periods are often preceded by heavy liquidation of long positions by traders wishing to avoid having to accept gold or "warehouse receipts."

Depository Receipt: *See* Warehouse receipt.

Dental Gold: Usually an alloy of gold containing 62.5 to 83.3 percent gold, plus (to increase the hardness of the alloy) some combination of silver, platinum, palladium, copper, and/or zinc.

Diamond Drilling: One type of drilling by mining companies to attain ore samples using a hollow diamond-studded bit that cuts out a rock core. A column of rock is extracted from inside the drill rod for geological examination and "assay."

Disseminated Ore: Ore in which small particles of gold or other valuable minerals are spread more or less uniformly throughout the deposit. This is in contrast to "massive ore" in which the gold or other valuable minerals are concentrated in almost solid form.

Dore or Dore Bar: An unrefined bullion bar of gold and silver which is often produced at a gold mine and shipped to a refiner to be upgraded into "good delivery bars." Dore is often about 65 percent gold and 35 percent silver.

Double Eagle: The U.S. $20 gold coin which was minted from 1849 through 1933. The coin was 0.900 fine and had a gold content of 0.9675 troy ounces. An "Eagle" was a $10 gold coin, which explains why the $20 coin was called a Double Eagle.

Ducat: Ducats were gold and silver coins which circulated in a number of European countries, as early as 1140. In recent years, the Austrian National Mint has made "restrikes" of Austro-Hungarian 1- and 4-Ducat coins.

Eagle: The first "legal tender" gold "bullion coin" minted by the United States beginning in 1795. This circulating gold coin was periodically reissued until 1933 with varying designs and weights. Quarter, Half, and "Double Eagles" were also minted. Beginning in 1986, the United States issued a new series of one-ounce, half-ounce, quarter-ounce, and tenth-ounce Eagle bullion coins. These investment coins are 0.9167 fine (22 karat) and carry nominal face values of $50, $20, $10, and $5, respectively.

Electrolytic Refining: The most efficient method of separating gold from ore or other metals. Using this method, it is possible to produce gold that is 0.9999 pure.

Electroplating: The deposition of gold on silver or a base metal by means of electrolysis. Electroplating is often used to plate costume jewelry and other items, as well as coat contact points in the electronics industry.

Epithermal Deposits: Gold deposits found at or near the earth's surface mainly in veins. These deposits were formed when hydrothermal fluids passed through the heated rocks of a volcanic system, depositing gold-containing minerals as the fluids cooled near the surface.

Exchange for Physicals or EFPs: The transfer of long futures positions for actual gold bullion prior to the futures contract "delivery date." EFPs are used by dealers to adjust their positions in physical and futures markets without changing their net positions.

Exchange Stocks: Physical gold bullion which is owned by futures market participants and which is held in exchange-approved warehouses. This gold is available for delivery; futures exchanges regularly report the quantity of gold held in approved warehouses.

Exercise Price: *See* Strike price.

Fabrication Demand: The demand for gold for use by various manufacturing industries including jewelry, electronics, dental, and other commercial uses as opposed to demand from investors and central banks.

FCM: *See* Futures Commission Merchant.

50-Peso: A Mexican gold coin. *See also* Centenario.

Fill or Kill: An order on a gold futures exchange that must be executed immediately, if possible, by the floor broker, or canceled.

Fine, Fineness, or Fine Gold: The purity of gold bars, coins, and alloys is defined as parts per 1000. "Four nines"—gold of 0.9999 fineness—contains 0999.9 parts per thousand and is considered the purest form of bullion. A gold bar of 0.995 fineness is 99.5 percent pure and contains 0.5 percent of some other metal. *See* Karat, which is a common measure of fineness.

Fine Ounce: A "troy ounce" of gold of at least 0.995 "fineness," unless otherwise specified.

Fixing: In the London gold market the price is set twice daily at 10:30 A.M. and 3:00 P.M. at a meeting of the five major bullion dealing firms. The fix, or price agreed upon by the dealers, is the price at which all of the buy and sell orders received by the five dealers from their customers can be matched up, clearing the market. Dealers in several other market centers—including Zurich and Paris—conduct their own local fixings. But the London fixing has become a benchmark price used for many transactions around the world.

Floor Broker: A trader actually working on the floor of a futures exchange executing orders received from a brokerage firm.

Fool's Gold: Iron pyrite, a mineral which looks like gold and has fooled many prospectors.

Forward Contract: An agreement similar to a "futures contract," for delivery of gold on some specified future date. A forward contract is entered upon directly between the buyer and seller and is not the result of trading on a futures exchange.

Forward Premium: The difference between the current price for physical gold and the price for future or forward delivery. In the gold market, the forward premium is often called the "contango," and reflects the "carrying charge" less the "gold lease rate."

Four Nines: Gold of the highest purity containing at least 999.9 parts per thousand gold. (Actually, certain uses by the electronics and other high-technology industries requires gold that has been refined to still higher standards.) Four nines gold is 24 karat. *See also* Fine, Fineness, Fine Gold, and Karat.

Fundamental Analysis: An approach to understanding market behavior based on trends in gold supply and demand in contrast to "technical analysis" which relies on past price performance as a guide to future price movements.

Futures Contract: An agreement reached on the floor of an organized gold futures exchange, like "COMEX" or "TOCOM," for example, calling for the "delivery" of a specified amount of gold at a specified time in the future and at an agreed upon price. Delivery must be at an exchange-approved warehouse.

Futures Commission Merchant (FCM): A brokerage house in the United States licensed by the "Commodity Futures Trading Commission" to conduct business on regulated futures markets.

Futures Exchange or Futures Market: A membership association organized to facilitate the trading of "futures contracts." The major futures markets for gold are "COMEX" in New York and "TOCOM" in Tokyo, but their are also gold futures exchanges in Hong Kong, Sidney, and Sao Paulo.

Gold Certificate: A certificate attesting to a person's ownership of gold in a depository or warehouse, often issued by banks and brokerage firms as an alternative to physical delivery of bullion to their clients. A gold certificate should specify the exact quantity and location of the underlying bullion.

Gold Dust: Fine particles of gold, often obtained by the mining of "placer" deposits.

Gold Equivalent: Gold mining companies with silver by-product often report their silver output in gold equivalent ounces. Occasionally, other metal by-products may also be reported in gold equivalent ounces. Silver quantities are converted in their gold equivalent using the current ratio of gold-to-silver prices. *See also* Gold/silver ratio.

Gold Filled: A layer of gold bonded to a base alloy and rolled or drawn to a prescribed thickness, often used in the manufacture of costume jewelry and other personal items, such as pens, pencils, lighters, etc. To meet U.S. regulatory standards, the gold must be at least 10 karat and its total weight must be at least one-twentieth of the total metal weight of the item. If the weight of the karat gold is less than one-twentieth, the item is designated as rolled "gold plate."

Gold Leaf or Gold Foil: Gold hammered to an extremely thin consistency—often no more than three-millionths of an inch—and used mostly for a variety of decorative purposes.

Gold Plate: A technique using electrolysis or mechanical bonding to deposit a thin layer of gold on a base metal alloy. Also known as gold overlay or rolled gold plate.

Gold/Silver Ratio: The number of ounces of silver that can be purchased with one ounce of gold calculated by dividing the price of gold by the price of silver.

Gold Standard: Various monetary systems based on the convertibility of currency into gold.

Good Delivery Bar: Bars that meet the standards of certain futures exchanges or market associations for delivery against short futures positions or to fulfill a physical sale. In the London market, good delivery bars are 350 to 430 troy ounces, with a minimum 0.995 "fineness," bearing the mark of an approved refiner. The "London Bullion Market Association" also requires that the bars be easy to handle and stack, and of good appearance. On "COMEX," either three "kilo bars" or one 100-ounce bar of 0.995 fineness and with a weight tolerance of plus or minus 5 percent may be delivered against a short futures contract. The bars must be cast by an approved refiner with the exact weight, fineness, bar number, and identifying stamp of the refiner clearly incised on each bar.

Good Till Canceled: An order to a broker or dealer which remains valid until it is fulfilled by the right price being achieved or until it is canceled.

Grade: The amount of gold (or other metal) per metric ton of ore, usually expressed in grams per ton or hundredths of an ounce per ton.

Grain: The earliest weight unit for gold, originally equivalent to one grain of wheat or barley. Now equal to 0.0648 "grams" or 0.002083 "troy ounces."

Gram: The basic unit of weight in the metric system. One kilogram equals 1000 grams. One gram is equivalent to 0.032 "troy ounces" or 15.43 "grains."

Grantor: The seller or "writer" of an option on gold bullion, mining equities, or futures contracts.

Grey Gold: An alloy of gold with some palladium and/or silver, and sometimes a little iron. Also called "white gold."

Gross Weight: The total weight of a gold bar or coin including any alloying metals as opposed to the weight of its "fine gold" content.

Hallmark: A mark or markings on gold, silver, or platinum jewelry (or other items) indicating its "fineness" and often other information including the producer and year of manufacture.

Heap Leaching: A process used by the mining industry for the extraction of gold and other metals from ores. Crushed ore is piled into large mounds covering several acres and a liquid cyanide solution is continuously sprinkled on the top of the heap. As the solution percolates through the ore, the gold is dissolved and later recovered from the collected solution.

Hedging: The use of various strategies often involving futures contracts, options, or forward sales agreements to offset the risk of price changes in the marketplace. A mine can hedge against a declining gold price by forward selling at a predetermined price some portion of its future production. An industrial user of gold can hedge against a price rise by buying forward or futures contracts to lock in his raw material costs.

Ingot: Originally a "good delivery bar," but today more generally any marketable gold (or silver) bar.

Initial Margin: The first payment made on the purchase or sale of a commodity futures contract as evidence of good faith and as a financial guarantee that the contract obligations will be fulfilled. *See* Margin.

In-the-Money: A "call option" is said to be in-the-money when its "strike price" is lower than the current market price of the underlying asset. A "put option" is in-the-money when the strike price is above the price of the underlying asset.

Intrinsic Value: The amount by which an option is "in-the-money." An option which is not in the money has no intrinsic value.

Karat: A measure of gold's purity or "fineness." The word originates from the ancient Greek word karation and the Arabic word qirat meaning fruit of the carob tree. Carob seeds were used in ancient markets as standard weights. 24-karat gold is pure gold of at least 0.99 fineness. 22-karat gold consists of 22 parts gold and 2 parts other metals; it is 22/24 pure gold or 0.9167 fine and is favored for jewelry in the Middle East and Far East. 18-karat gold is 18/24 pure or 0.750 fineness; this is the legal minimum purity in Italy and France for an item to be designated as gold. 14-karat gold is 14/24 pure or 0.583 fine; this is the popular purity of jewelry in the United States.

Karat Gold: In the United States gold of not less than 10-karat fineness.

Kilobar: A gold bar weighing one kilogram or 32.1507 "troy ounces." Kilobars of 0.9999 fineness are a popular bar size for investors and jewelry fabricators in many Asian countries. In the United States, three kilobars of at least 0.995 fineness are deliverable against one 100-ounce gold futures contract.

Krugerrand: The first gold bullion coin, minted in South Africa beginning in 1967 and marketed internationally since 1970. Krugerrands are 22 karat, or 0.9167 fine. These coins are legal tender without face value. At first, minted only in units containing exactly 1 troy ounce of fine gold, fractional coins of half-ounce, quarter-ounce, and tenth-ounce denominations were introduced in later years. The coin fell into disfavor beginning in 1984 when a number of important countries enacted anti-South African sanctions which, among other things, prohibited importation of this coin into their domestic markets. This import ban lasted until 1991. Over the years, more than 44 million krugerrands were minted.

Lakh: An Indian word for 100,000 ounces. Now the term is often used by traders and dealers to describe silver and, occasionally, gold orders of this size.

Legal Tender: Coins officially minted and legally acceptable as a means of payment. In recent years, beginning with the Krugerrand in 1967, countries producing "bullion coins" have designated them as official legal tender even though they are not used as a means of payment. Originally, legal tender status for bullion coins made them exempt from sales taxes in certain countries or localities.

Leverage: The ability to control an investment whose market value is a multiple of one's actual cash investment. Gold futures are leveraged because the investor may only pay "initial margin" of 5 or 10 percent of the contract's full value. Similarly, the "premium" paid on an option is only a fraction of the value of the underlying asset. Equities purchased on margin are leveraged for the same reason. Sometimes leverage also refers to the degree of price volatility of gold mining shares in relationship to a change in the underlying price of gold. In Britain and South Africa, this sensitivity of gold equity prices to changes in the price of gold bullion is called gearing.

Leverage Contract: A contract sold by a retail bullion dealer requiring a down payment usually of 20 to 25 percent of the total value of the gold. The retailer finances the balance and charges interest and storage. The bullion remains with the dealer as collateral.

Limit Move, Limit Up or Down: The maximum price by which a futures contract may change, up or down, in one trading day. On "COMEX," the daily limit for gold is $25; if the price moves by its limit for two consecutive days, the limit is raised by 50 percent.

Limit Order: An order specifying a maximum buying price ("bid") or minimum selling price ("ask"); in contrast to a "market order" which is to be executed immediately without regard to price.

Liquidation: Closing out a futures market or options position prior to contract maturity.

Liquid Gold: A solution of gold and other chemicals used in the decorative arts and certain high-technology applications.

Local: An independent floor trader on a commodity futures exchange who trades principally for his own account.

London Fix or London Price: *See* Fixing.

London Bullion Market Association: A self-regulating association of London gold dealers established in 1987 to represent the interests of the local gold dealing community and to promulgate technical and ethical rules of conduct.

Long: A purchase in physical, futures, options, or equities markets usually in expectation of a price rise. Also, someone—a miner, refiner, or jewelry manufacturer—holding an unhedged position. *See also* Short.

Maple Leaf: A series of gold "legal tender" "bullion coins" issued by Canada's Royal Canadian Mint. First minted in 1979, the coin is now available in one-ounce as well as half-, quarter-, and tenth-ounce sizes. The Maple Leaf was the first "four nines," 24-karat bullion coin.

Margin: In futures markets, good-faith funds put up as collateral to guarantee contract fulfillment; *See also* Initial margin and Variation margin. In equity markets, the partial payment—usually 50 percent of the stock purchase price—with the brokerage firm lending its customers the balance.

Margin Call: A request from a broker for additional funds in order to raise the cash position back up to minimum levels after an adverse price move on futures or equities markets.

Market Order: An order to buy or sell bullion, futures contracts, options, or equities immediately at the best available price.

Medals and Medallions: "Commemorative coins" or "rounds" issued by a government or private mint without "legal tender" status.

Metal Account: Some banks and bullion dealers offer accounts denominated in ounces of gold rather than dollars or other currency units. Metal account holdings may be "unallocated" liabilities of the bank, that is, not backed by specific bars or other assets.

Metallurgy: The science of metals and alloys. Process metallurgy is concerned with the extraction of metals from their ores and with the refining of metals and alloys.

Metric Ton or Tonne: In the metric system, the unit of weight equal to 1000 "kilograms" or 32,150.7 "troy ounces." A *metric ton* is equivalent to 2204.61 pounds. A *short ton* is a unit of the avoirdupois system equal to 2000 pounds.

Mexican Peso: *See* Centenario.

Mine Life: The number of years an active gold mine can continue economic production at current rates of output before its reserves are depleted. Estimates of mine life are sometimes based on actual "proven reserves" and "probable reserves" or may be only an approximate estimate.

Moving Average: In "technical analysis," moving averages of daily prices are used to smooth out the daily price fluctuations in order to chart the underlying price trend. Technicians define buy or sell signals when daily or short-term moving average prices cross a longer-term moving average on a price chart.

Naked Option: The sale of a "put" or "call" option on bullion, mining shares, futures contracts, or other assets by someone not owning the underlying asset.

Napoleon: A French, 20-franc, gold coin first minted in 1803 and bearing the likeness of Napoleon I and, later, Napoleon III. Later, this term became the generic description of subsequent French gold coins of varying designs.

Nearby Delivery: The listed trading month on a futures exchange closest to the present calender month.

Nugget: Chunks of gold usually washed from rock and found mainly in alluvial deposits or river beds. Nuggets are often valued for their natural beauty as well as their gold content and are frequently bought by collectors or used in jewelry. The largest known nugget, dubbed the Welcome Stranger and weighing 2284 ounces, was discovered in Australia in 1858. The "Australia Nugget" is also the brand name of the bullion coin series produced by that country.

Numismatic Coin: A coin that is valued by collectors and investors because of its rarity and its esthetic, cultural, or historical appeal rather than its metal content. In contrast, "bullion coins" are valued for their gold or silver content.

Obverse: The side of a coin bearing the principal design, in contrast to the "reverse."

Offer: *See* Bid.

Onza: A Mexican, 0.900 fine (21.6 karat) bullion coin containing 1 ounce of fine gold. First minted in 1981, the coin has never been successfully marketed.

Open Pit, Open Cut or Open Face: A method of mining gold or other minerals which are deposited on or close to the earth's surface by simply excavating a large pit. Many of the newer mines in North America and Australia utilize this low-cost method for mining low-grade ores.

Open Interest: On a commodity futures or options exchange, the number of outstanding contracts or positions which have not been offset or liquidated either by opposite transactions or by delivery of the underlying asset. Open interest is an important measure of market liquidity, often used with other statistics by "technical analysts" for clues about prospective price changes.

Open Outcry: The method of trading on "COMEX" and many other commodity futures exchanges by calling out the "bid" or "ask" price, contract month, and number of contracts.

Operating Cost: The cost of mining gold, usually expressed in dollars (or other currency units) per ounce. Precise definitions may vary from one company to the next. *See also* Cash production cost.

Option: An option gives the holder the right, but not the obligation, to buy or sell a gold futures contract, mining equity, bullion, or other asset. The grantor or writer of the option is obligated to buy or sell the underlying asset at a predetermined price at the request of the option holder. *See also Call, Grantor, Premium, Put, and Writer*

Ore Reserves: The amount of mineral-bearing rock which can be exploited economically to yield gold or other minerals, usually designated in tons and "grade." Reserves may be proven, probable, or possible depending on the amount of quantifiable evidence from drilling and other tests available to calculate the tonnage and gold content.

Original Margin: *See* Initial margin.

Out-of-the-Money: Refers to "put options" where the "strike price" is lower than the current market price of the underlying asset, or "call options" where the strike price is higher than that of the underlying asset. *See also* In-the-money.

Ounce: *See* Troy ounce.

Panda: A series of 0.9999 fine gold "bullion coins" issued by the China Mint in Beijing in 1-ounce and fractional units. Because the coins are minted to half-proof quality and have new designs each year, the earlier issues have become collectors' items.

Paper Gold: Futures and forward contracts, options, certificates, storage accounts, and other forms of gold ownership not necessitating the physical delivery of bullion or coins.

Penny Stock: A low-priced, often speculative stock issue, usually under $2 a share.

Pennyweight: A unit of weight equal to one-twentieth of a "troy ounce." Originally, the weight of an early English silver penny weighing 24 troy "grains."

Philharmonic or Philharmoniker: A series of one-ounce, quarter-ounce, and tenth-ounce 0.9999 fine (24 karat), gold "bullion coins" issued by the Austrian mint beginning in 1989. With a face value of 2000 shillings, these legal tender coins honor the Vienna Philharmonic Orchestra.

Physicals: Gold bullion bars or coins, as opposed to futures or forward contracts; also known as "actuals."

Pit: The area on the floor of a futures exchange where trading takes place; sometimes called the "ring."

Placer or Placer Deposit: A concentration of gold or other precious metals in the form of "nuggets" or particles that have accumulated alluvially in river beds or near the seashore through the process of weathering and erosion.

Plumb Gold: A gold alloy which assays exactly (or plumb) to the "karat" stamped on the product.

Porphyry Gold: A deposit in which gold-bearing crystals occur in finely disseminated grains or in veinlets throughout the ore body.

Premium: In the bullion coin and bar market, the difference between the price paid for the item and the current market value of its "fine gold" content. This premium is a reflection of manufacturing as well as distribution costs and, at times, scarcity value in the market. In the futures markets, an additional payment specified by exchange rules for the delivery of gold bars exceeding 0.995 fineness. In the options market, the price paid for the option.

Proof or Proof Coin: A high-quality coin struck from specially prepared dies and usually sold to collectors at a substantial premium over the price of an ordinary coin. Proof versions of many of the popular "bullion coins" are issued each year in limited mintages.

Put or Put Option: A contract giving its buyer (or option holder) the right, but not the obligation, to sell bullion, equities, or futures contracts at a specified price (the "strike price") on or before a specified date. The seller or "grantor" of the option is obligated to accept the underlying asset if requested by the option holder. Upon entering into an options contract the holder pays the grantor a fee or "premium" for the right to make the subsequent sale.

Rand: The currency unit of South Africa, the largest national mine producer of gold.

Recycled Gold: *See* Scrap.

Red Gold: An "alloy" of gold, silver, and copper, which imparts a red tone to the metal; occasionally, a red gold alloy may also contain some zinc.

Refractory Ore: Gold-bearing ore in which the precious metal is encapsulated with sulfides or other minerals making the extraction process difficult and expensive.

Reserves: *See* Ore reserves.

Resting Order: An order to buy or sell futures, options, or equities to be executed at a given price point. Also known as a standing order.

Restrike: A new minting of an out-of-date coin using the original dies. A number of countries issue restrikes of old gold coins. Typically minted in quantities sufficient to meet any current demand, these are usually sold at a low premium over their gold content value. The "Austrian Corona," for example, is a popular restrike among gold investors.

Reverse: The back side of a coin. *See also* Obverse.

Ring: The official trading area on the floor of the London Metal Exchange. *See also* Pit.

Rolled Gold: Often equivalent to "gold filled," except in the United States where the proportion of gold alloy to the weight of the entire item may be less than 1/20th, but the "fineness" of the gold may not be less than 10 "karat."

Rolling Forward or Rolling Over: In futures and options markets, the liquidation of a position in a nearby month for an equivalent position in a later month.

Round-Turn: Commissions to commodity brokers, unlike stockbrokers, generally are quoted on a round-turn basis, that is the commission includes both the initial purchase and the subsequent liquidation of the position.

Scrap: Material from old jewelry, electronics and telecommunications equipment, and other gold-bearing items which is sent to a refiner in order to recover and recycle the metal content.

Secondary Supply: Gold recovered from "scrap," refined, and fabricated into bars for sale in the physical market.

Settlement Price: Often referred to as the closing price, the settlement price is the price set at the close of trading each day for every listed contract month on a futures exchange by the settlement committee. This price is the basis for determining "margin" calls by the "clearing-house."

Short: In the futures market, someone holding a contract to sell a commodity such as gold; may also be used as an adjective to describe a trader's position, or a verb to describe selling of a commodity for future delivery. In the equity market, someone who has sold borrowed stock in the expectation of repurchasing the shares at a lower price before they must be returned to the owner. Generally, anyone with an obligation to deliver gold or other assets in the future.

Solid Gold: In the United States, the Federal Trade Commission defines solid gold as any article that does not have a hollow center and has a "fineness" of "10 karat" or higher.

Sovereign: *See* British Sovereign.

Spot or Spot Price: The price of gold for immediate delivery in the physical market, which usually means two business days after the transaction date. In futures markets, spot refers to the price for the current delivery month.

Spread: The difference between a market makers bid and ask price for gold, equities, or other assets. Sometimes, a spread may refer to opposite positions taken in gold and silver markets to profit from a change in the "gold/silver ratio." *See also* Straddle.

Standing Order: *See* Resting order.

Stops or Stop-Loss Orders: A "resting order" to liquidate a gold futures market position at a certain price point. Stops are used to limit losses should the market price move against a trader's position.

Straddle: Futures market trading strategies, also known as a "spread," involving the purchase of a contract for one delivery month and the sale of a contract for another delivery month. In options markets, the simultaneous holding of "puts" and "calls" for the same underlying asset. Spreads or straddles may also be established using a futures position and an options contract.

Strike Price: The predetermined price at which an "option" may be exercised and the underlying asset bought (in the case of a "call") or sold (in the case of a "put"). Also known as the "exercise price."

Swap: In the physical market a location swap is the exchange of bullion in one location for gold in another location; a quality swap is the exchange of gold bars of differing purity. In recent years, a swap has also described the simultaneous sale of physical gold and the repurchase of a like quantity for future delivery. This transaction has been used by central banks as a means of raising short-term finance without permanent sales of official reserves. In futures and options markets, swaps are used to "roll forward" or "roll over" a position from one contract month to another later month; also known as a "switch."

Tael: A Chinese unit of weight equal to 1.20337 "troy ounces" or 37.429 "grams." Bars of 1-, 5-, and 10-tael weights are popular in many Asian countries, and in Hong Kong, the Gold and Silver Exchange trades futures contracts in 100-tael denominations.

Tailings: The waste material from ore after metallurgical extraction of gold or other metals. In recent years, improved extraction techniques allow the retreatment of old tailings dumps to economically recover additional gold.

Technical Analysis: The use of historical price, open interest, and volume statistics and charts to study a market's past performance and forecast its future price prospects.

Technical Analyst: A practitioner of "technical analysis."

Ten Tola Bar: *See* Tola.

Time Value: The amount by which an "option's" "premium" exceeds its "intrinsic value." Time value reflects the amount of time remaining before the option matures as well as the price volatility of the underlying asset.

TOCOM or Tokyo Commodity Exchange: The principal commodity futures exchange in Japan, trading contracts for delivery of one "kilobar" of 0.9999 fine gold.

Tola: A standard unit of weight in India and Pakistan equal to 0.375 "troy ounces" or 11.1 "grams." Ten tola gold bars of 0.999 "fineness" are popular on the Indian subcontinent and also in the Persian Gulf region.

Ton or Tonne: *See* Metric ton.

Trading Limit: The maximum daily price change permitted by exchange rules in a single trading session on a futures market. Also the maximum number of futures contracts, according to "CFTC" regulations, which may be bought or sold by one speculator.

Troy Ounce: A standard unit of weight for gold, and popular the world over as the basic unit for quoting the price of 0.995 "fine" gold. Its name is derived from the unit of weight used during the Middle Ages at the annual fair in Troyes, France. One troy ounce equals 31.1034807 "grams," 480 "grains," or 20 "pennyweights." 32.1507 troy ounces equals 1 "kilogram."

Unallocated or Unallocated Gold: Metal which is held by a bank or bullion dealer on behalf of its clients in a common pool, without assigning ownership of individual bars. Unallocated gold may be an unsecured liability of a bullion bank backed by gold loans or other assets, rather than by physical metal held in their own vaults. *See also* Allocated.

Variation Margin: Additional margin that an investor must deposit with his broker (usually within 24 hours) if the market price moves against his position, or that a brokerage firm must deposit with the "clearinghouse" (usually within one hour) if the market price moves against the net position of the firm's clients.

Volume: The total number of contracts or shares traded within a given period on a commodity futures exchange or stock market. Volume is used in conjunction with other statistics as an indicator of market mood or interest by "technical analysts."

Vreneli: A 20-franc, Swiss gold coin minted from 1897 until 1949 of 0.900 "fineness," and containing 0.1867 "troy ounces." Today, these coins remain popular with Swiss gold investors and often trade at a premium of more than 20 percent above their gold content value.

Wafer: A small, flat bullion bar often less than 50 "grams" in weight and popular among investors in Asia and the Middle East.

Warehouse Receipt: Also known as a depository receipt, a document specifying the quantity, fineness, and location of gold held in a depository on behalf of the holder of the receipt. Exchange of these receipts often substitutes for moving physical metal to satisfy the delivery requirements of gold futures contracts.

White Gold: Gold which has been "alloyed" with various combinations of platinum, palladium, nickel, copper, zinc, and/or silver to alter its color and hardness for jewelry applications, especially gem settings.

Writer: The seller or "grantor" of an "options" contract. In return for a payment from the option holder, the writer is obliged to accept, at the request of the holder, the underlying asset at a predetermined price at any time up until the contract expires.

Yellow Gold: An alloy of gold, silver, and copper and sometimes zinc intended to make the metal look yellower than natural gold itself.

Yellow Metal: A nickname or slang term for gold used to distinguish it from the red metal (copper) or the white metals (platinum, palladium, or silver).

Index

Political tension, as factor affecting gold
     prices, 58
Political upheaval, gold as security from, 4
Porphyry gold, 204
Portfolio, 3, 149-151
     diversifier, gold as a, 155
     enhancement, gold and, 149-151
     hedge, gold as a, 3, 150
Portfolios, gold, 147-152. See also Gold
     plated portfolio
Position taking, day trading vs., 130-131
Position trades, definition, 130
Premium, 74-76, 136, 205
     definition of options, 136
     some considerations in coin purchase,
        76
     the coin market and, 74-75
Price, 57-58, 62, 139
     appreciation, as only return on gold in-
        vestment, 57-58
     fixing, 62
     levels, as factor in growth of jewelry de-
        mand, 41
     quote, sample, 139
     risk, mining shares and, 91
     sensitivity, mines and 92
     table, futures, how to read, 124-125
        reading the options, 139-140
     trends, understanding for profit, 129
     volatility, options, 137
Price-to-earnings ratio, mining shares and,
     94
Pricing, options, definition, 136-137
Private ownership, effects on gold market,
     56
Project development loans, as factor in
     bear market, 16
Proof coin, 205
Pure gold investment, as advantage in
     coins, 70-71
Puts, definition, 136, 205
Pyramid, investment, 151

Rand, South African, 8, 205
     vs. gold 1975-1991 (chart), 8
Rate of return, calculating, 57-58
Real interest rates vs. gold prices 1976-
     1991 (chart), 60
Real time, definition, 130
Rectangles, as chart formation, 171-174

Recycled gold, 205
Red gold, definition, 205
Refractory ore, definition, 205
Resaleability, coins, 71
Reserves, 49, 50-51, 205
     as a percent of total reserves (chart), 50-
        51
     distribution of, 49
     gold as a proportion of, 51
Resting order, 205
Restrikes, definition, 70, 205
Reversals, spotting key using technical
     analysis, 169
Reverse head and shoulders patterns,
     170-171
Ring, definition, 205
Risk-averse portfolio, gold as ingredient
     in, 4
Risks, 4, 73-75, 91-92, 111-113, 206
     diversifying against in coin market, 73-
        75
     mining share investments and, 91-92
     mutual funds and, 111-113
     reducing with gold, 4
Rolled gold, definition, 206
Round turn, definition, 206
Rules for investing, 161-162
Runaway gap, chart formation, 176

Safety, as factor in holding gold reserves,
     52
Sales tax, coins and, 75
Savings, tradition of gold as, 41
Scalping, definition, 131
Scrap recovery, 16-17, 23, 33-34, 206
Secondary supply, 33-34, 206
     definition, 206
     See also Scrap recovery
Sector demands, official, *see* Official sector
     demands
Security, as factor in holding gold re-
     serves, 52
Settlement price, 125, 206
Short positions, representation of, 124,
     206
Short-term holder, as type of gold inves-
     tor, 156
Slopes, as chart formation, 174
Smuggling, 56
Solid gold, 206

About the Author

Jeffrey Nichols is president of American Precious Metals
Advisors and the publisher of *Metals Fax*. He has consulted
for major gold mining companies, bullion dealers, the
World Gold Council, the Austrian and Royal Canadian
Mints and several gold-oriented mutual funds. In addition,
he is a director of Dickenson Mines Ltd., a gold and
industrial minerals producer, and a past director of the
American Stock Exchange's commodities subsidiary. He is
past president of the International Precious Metals Institute.